The Winning Link

The Winning Link

A lesson on how winners thrive with their talents, dreams and passions

Michael E. Salako

YOUCAXTON PUBLICATIONS

OXFORD & SHREWSBURY

For

Jaaziel, Adiya, & Hephzibah

gems of inestimable value.

Contents

About this Book

This book tells the story of you and me. It is about how each one of us makes his or her own little contribution to the world. It is not about dreaming small but about standing tall.

Solomon, acclaimed by many to be the wisest and richest man in history once said, 'he who treasures understanding will soon prosper'. Study this little book and find practical and proven lessons on how mankind, throughout history, has been in constant search of meaning and purpose. Discover how, by ordinary, everyday means, peoples' lives have been positively transformed and how, with similar ordinary thoughts or means, we too can live up to the demands and expectations of our time and give meaning to our lives.

This book began more than a decade ago in group discussions with friends on how to make a little difference and how to be fulfilled – and how one can do this when it seems that all one has is nothing.

Preface

If you were the only one to benefit from this book, I would be most satisfied with my achievement. I wrote it to answer unfulfilled longings that I had observed among a number of people from all spheres of life. Hardly anyone with a reasonable capacity can expect to pass through life without entering one or more such unfulfilled phases, although some manage it better than others. On this basis, this work aims to reassure you that everything good is possible by bringing to the fore, as in flashes, salient lessons and examples of everyday success.

These small lessons, which seem ordinary and unimportant, provide us with lessons and, for those who take note, they have the power to create a turnaround for the individual as well as his/her enterprise if they have one. In this book there are lessons from success and lessons from failure – since reflection on the errors of others can sometimes provide a safeguard against pitfalls and thereby improve how you move towards your own areas of strength and mission.

You will note that I emphasise – regardless of how the world defines success, be it as big houses, big cars, big four, big five, big-data and the likes – that if you stay strong, even when the green leaves wither, and if you constantly engage your own personal judgement as to what actions or choices present you with the best possibility of true worth and happiness, you will at all times provide yourself with the basis for a memorable livelihood.

And no one can define what that is for you.

This work does not dwell on arguments surrounding the true nature of morals, ethics or happiness. It simply reminds you that, even if you live to be a hundred, the time is too short to spend in waiting anxiously to attain your next big status in the world or in waiting equally aimlessly in search of opportunities that do not arrive; not when you can start living purposefully right now, by making yourself alive and shining forth that little light within you.

By your 'little lights' I mean little kernels of knowledge that you can further enhance, or little words of inspiration that can act on your mind, or even small actions that enliven others. Your little lights or treasures are also your passion for a worthy cause or your special gift in a field of interest – and the list goes on.

Tapping into these timeless treasures has resulted in this publication. It is divided into three small parts, and each part builds on the last, so a little more focus is required as you read through the parts.

I wish you joy and happiness in life.

Michael E. Salako
London, 2014

Acknowledgements

Only grace furnished this book and, for this, my profound gratitude goes to the Almighty God.

A special thanks goes to the management and staff of YouCaxton Publications: You made sure that the publishing process was not cumbersome.

Because this book reflects the contributions of different people whose values have helped me to understand how I desire all experience happiness, freedom and fulfilment to be, I affirm that writing this book would have been impossible if our paths had never crossed.

It pains me that it is almost impossible to mention all the names of people in this category. However, it would be lazy of me not to tender my appreciation to Dr. Williams Akerele, who read through the first manuscript some years back and gave his recommendation. In like manner, my appreciation goes to my uncle, Mr. Bayo Adeleke for his help and guidance.

To my Mum, thanks for always believing in me, because not all mothers believe in the work of their children. To Dad, for your prayers, and to Funmi, Wumi and Seun, my siblings and their spouses, I can't thank you all enough. Thanks to

Mr. Benjamin Olosinmo for going through the manuscript and making recommendations, thanks also for the words of encouragement from your friend, Mr Ayinde Sulaimon.

To Adeola Oyenubi and Niyi Otunuga, for all the times I demanded that we held discussions on dreams; to Ojealero Isemede, who knows no other slogan than 'living the dream', thanks for all your comments on the manuscript. Also, thanks to Adesola Adewale, Noushin Afrashteh, Dr. Monisola Ogunsanya, Omolara Oyediran, Benneth Orgu, Olubusola Ojo, Anthonia Johnson, Margaret Ogunrotimi, Cat Lewis, Yul Hechanova, Nathalie Shango, Bukky Okelana, Blessing Okpala, Ayinde Saheed, Francisca Mensah, and Ola Abimbola for all your contributions in words and actions that made this work possible.

Part A

Strands of Treasure

Chapter 1

Dare to Learn

The real deal is the sincere heart that strives to learn and improve itself for the benefit of society.

Regardless of the numerous opportunities that life offers us, it is a known fact that no one can outwit life, unless it is by creating a good legacy earned in the school of life. The world has oftentimes been compared to a market place rather than to a school, but nobody stays in the market for ever and so it is also with schools. In a marketplace, people buy and sell, but the shared benefit of their engagement cannot be much relied on except when feedback is provided, and usually buyer and seller go their separate ways unenlightened about the value-creation process. In a school however, both learners and instructors can participate effectively and come up with practical and lasting solutions to the problems they face, or create new products or designs.

And, if it is true that a good legacy is an end result that only becomes evident after one is long gone, then, at the very least, a *potential* legacy waits for us and it can be made real through our contribution to the world. But to achieve this, there is a need for us to put on our learning cap and find meaning from every possible thing around us.

'Yellow gold has its price', a Chinese proverb says, 'but learning is priceless'.

An old story of a boy who attempted to understand nature but unintentionally disproved it, demonstrates our need for learning. Noticing that it was only after the geese sat on their laid eggs that they became mothers, young Thomas Edison got hold of some newly-laid eggs and sat on them for a length of time to see if they would hatch. They did not of course and so he was disproved by nature.

What a stupid learner, you may say, but he *eventually* understood – and what he understood was that you can't disobey the laws of life and expect a miracle. Goethe, a naturalist noted: "nature understands no jesting, she is always right, and the errors and faults are always those of man. The man incapable of appreciating her, she despises, and only to the apt, the pure and the true does she resign herself and reveal her secrets."

As you likely know already, this 'stupid learner', Edison, was in the process of learning a basic law: that learning is lifelong and can arise equally from our errors as from our successes. And, of course, he kept on learning and, by trial and error, identified numerous ways that a viable commercial incandescent lamp *can't* be produced.

The story of the boy-cum-man, Thomas Edison, is echoed in the stories of numerous other achievers today, achievers who may, some of them, at one time, have been described as intelligent idiots.

You and I have learned about one of Edison's success stories. In his quest for discovering a means of illumination, his record remains unbeaten with regards to how he learned by 'failing forward'. Though he had but little formal education for a light, he yet illuminated his world through learning and was accepted as a leader among the inventors of his generation by others in the school of life, on account of all the inventions patented by him.

Learning brings illumination be it through thoughtfulness, by listening, or by other means. Nothing speaks as tenderly, yet securely, as learning. When the voice of learning is heard, insight arises. Ideas can be developed when the light of learning shines on them.

And true were the words of George Santayanna: "Knowledge of what is possible is the beginning of happiness". Barely a week after reviewing the original manuscript of this book, news emerged of a homeless man by the name of Leo Grand, who was asked by a benefactor if he would rather receive a $100 bill or take a computer-programming coaching session. He accepted the latter and, after just a few months of coaching, he developed an app that could help monitor CO_2 emission in automobiles, thus contributing to the fight against climate change.

Homelessness, poverty or other scary conditions are powerless to define a person who dares to value 'time for learning' as an intangible asset, something that guarantees a long-term reward. John Paul DeJoria, twice homeless and from a very rough background, eventually became co-founder of a multi-million dollar hair empire, the John Paul Mitchell Systems. For the space of one-and-a-half years, he went beyond his official duties at his former place of work in order to learn everything possible about business and he did this so as to contribute to the world.

Leo and Paul had treasures in them, but it was learning that brought their treasures to the world. In the light of these achievements, what a magnificent impact will learning have on our own lives when we consider what a great thing it is to learn?

It is a rapidly changing world, be it in business or any other field, and those constantly striving to learn, especially about things relevant to their own given areas of endeavour, will adapt and emerge as worthy participants in the race of life. What is more, consumer taste is now rapidly changing and the commercial practice of pushing wanted and unwanted products and services almost equally onto the market place has given room to marketing that uses targeted information that relates to customers' preferences and buying behaviour. He who is endowed with the right knowledge dictates the rules.

So what can we learn today?

Chapter 2

Defining Moments

The show is on, but the choice is yours.

The last chapter demonstrated the potential for making a fortune inherent in choosing to learn. Just as learning is a choice, choosing to live a meaningful life is also a choice. Making choices is similar to what we can observe in an open event, where people generally can be grouped as participants or spectators. And, all of life is like that – we become either participants or spectators by writing and reinforcing, daily, the stories of our lives through the choices we make. We can complain or choose to comply, but life demands results whatever we choose. It's all about our decisions; only our decisions propel actions.

Nylon has become an almost indispensable item of everyday convenience. It has greater strength than any natural fibre and is of great commercial value, being used for tyres, shoes, tooth brush, carpets, nets and swimwear among other things. The story of nylon's development shows us how problem-solving as a basis for research can be highly effective and it shows the power of the resolute mind. Before the start of World War II, tension with Japan, the world's then premier supplier of silk, obliged the United States to seek an alternative, in particular for the making of parachutes. In other words, the people of the United States refused to be written off as mere spectators when it came to the production of silk, despite having no silk industry worth speaking of their own. They were determined to be players. Their lack of silk led them to make a creative choice and their choice illustrates the popular but hard-to-chew phenomenon of 'opportunity in disguise'.

It all depends on how change is embraced. Choice creates change, and positive change can thrive, even in chaos.

By the exercise of choice, sometimes lives have been preserved and by it, also, employees have become employers.

Elsa Thomasma, was not the sort of person who was expert in Wall Street banking or International Development Studies, but in the face of a terrible calamity the beauty of her heart offered what even the richest of men could not likely offer, however clever and well-educated they might be.

She was able to propose in her mind what to do when she pondered on how to embark on the next season of her life. She considered how, each time any village was bombarded by the arrogant force of nature in the Philippines, at least one life was lost in that community. She volunteered and began fund raising for others to help build a shelter for an unknown young widow and her kid in a country far away from hers because she believed that people can reclaim authority over devastating natural forces by the choices that they make, be they planned, reactive, small or big. Elsa, who was at first thought to have been drowned and swept away by the turbulent storm, Typhoon Haiyan, which took more than six-thousand souls in a single sweep of villages and islands in the Philippines, prepared a sanctuary, like the historical Noah's ark, against the dreaded draconian storm, thereby limiting that monster's treacherous impact and, by doing so, redefined history by saving everybody in the village where she worked.

The lesson of Elsa Thomasma is that we too can choose to live purposefully, and that what at first may appear as a setback can be turned to our advantage and to the advantage of others.

To take another example of the power of choice, Natalie Massenet acted in the spirit of the popular view of economics credited to Lionel Robbins, which defines economics as: 'a science that studies human behaviour as a relationship between ends and scarce means which have alternative uses'. Natalie was a writer for a fashion firm when she responded to the call of destiny after she found herself challenged by a question posed on a bank leaflet, of all things.

"Are you someone that can turn opportunity to reality?" the leaflet seemed to ask.

Because of the question the leaflet posed, she *chose* to be an entrepreneur and founded an online fashion magazine that later evolved into the world's premier sensational fashion tale, 'Net a Porter', which caters for fashion enthusiasts, followers and employees across different regions of the world.

When we consider the ends, we look within; other than this, we look without. Therefore, by making valuable choices we can, in the long run, break the grip of full dependence on others. Man and time can be saved, jobs can be created, and money and materials can be multiplied, or possibly recycled or saved. To achieve these ends, we must learn to choose and to look (think) within our means, capacities or potentials, rather than complain powerlessly.

And that begs the question of what choices we can make

on the immediate or critical issues around us and how do we go about it? Charles E. Bennett once said: "making decisions is (should be) simple; get the facts, seek God's guidance, form a judgement, worry no more".

'Going about it' may not look as simple as Charles suggests, but he's right that it's all about choosing the right path rather than accepting the norms.

§

Notes from Lesson 1 and 2.

Though you may be error-prone and falter many a times, yet it is important that you learn how to be effective at making right *choices*. Likewise, choose to learn effectively.

Start now and, by all means, make a choice today.

Chapter 3

A Bargain's Break

Leading, as in winning, is to be sold out in self-sacrifice.

Leaders are not normally angels but show me a leader and I will show you a man or woman capable of great self-sacrifice. Winning may be for self-aggrandisement, but leading must, always, be for the end purposes of others also. Indeed, most or many inventors have had, as a prime motive behind their adventure, the desire to better the lot of others, to make others happy. Not all leaders are inventors, but people affected will often smile more because of the little extras a leader offers. Today, hardly any organization or individual can thrive long and better without adopting service excellence as a key component for goal attainment – and movement towards such a goal must be led by a leader.

There are so many examples of events in the lives of exemplary characters that demonstrate the effect of leaders that it's hard to know where to begin: Andrew Carnegie, Paul Getty, Bill Gates, Gandhi, Graham Bell, Henry Ford, Alfred Marshall, Aliko Dangote or Dwight Eisenhower to name but a few. Ike's chronicle seems best for our purposes.

Having attained a foremost position in the army and being about to complete his first US Presidential term, Ike canvassed for re-election while his opponent argued that Ike had been only a part time President because he was always falling sick during his first tenure. And yet, despite Ike's many absences, the people loved him and knew he was a man of virtue. He was re-elected.

This is not a political book, but Dwight Eisenhower is useful for us because of a life-virtue that he demonstrates. Ike was born to one of the poorest families in Abilene, Kansas, USA. When quite young, he agreed to work full-time at a creamery in order to pay for his brother's first-year college expenses, a noble deed. When his brother asked him for an additional year of support, Ike did not object. And later, for himself, looking within, opted for a free military college.

If there is lesson from this, it is that we need to go the extra mile for others as occasions demand.

While his support for his brother, when young, may seem easy to relate to, his responses to other encounters while in the army remain a question for debate among many business thinkers and philosophers but, through all this, he remained human and considerate of others and, for a considerable length of time, he remained on a military rank but didn't use that rank to seek better opportunities from the business world. Bernard Montgomery, a British Field Marshall, said of him: "his real strength lies in his human qualities".

It cannot be said that, in his formative years, Ike knew that he would one day be a president, but his childhood experience and the lessons that he learned at that time he took with him into adulthood, reflecting a soul that sought to protect the interests of those he cared for. Service excellence was in his genes.

Perhaps you are thinking that this sort of behaviour may only be of benefit to those seeking political leadership? Let's consider Theodore Vail. It has been said on many occasions: "Alexander Graham Bell invented the telephone and Theodore Vail invented the telephone business." Though different views persist on whether he was, as is widely accepted, a pioneer of the fluid concept of organizational service rather than of short-term profit as a yardstick for performance, there can be no doubt that his life embodies the 'fluid concept' as is shown by his career while formerly with US Railway Mail Service.

From the start, Theodore Vail had a mind-set beyond what he was employed for as a mail clerk. He began to initiate the development of the current mail-delivery system in the USA from when he first reported for duty. He saw ahead. He agreed to 'a cut in salary' with another employer, the Bell's System, the world's first telephony company, and he did this in order to take up a post that would enable him later to revolutionise the telephone industry by introducing the long-distance interconnectivity paradigm.

Furthermore, he established a comprehensive pension system in recognition of the contribution of the internal customers (employees) of the company and this shows his longing for the well-being of others. However, he understood that self-sacrifice is not self-depreciation and he resigned when he felt undermined by the decrepit organizational politics of the Bell's System – only to be recalled after some years, having by then proved himself through the tremendous impact of his many other business exploits during his stay away.

Leading, in any field, is not about going the extra mile but about genuine service while doing so.

There have been other such noble individuals in our own time, men such as Salman Khan of Khan Academy, who resigned from a high and lofty position as a hedge-fund trader in order to strengthen an online platform that he had created. This online platform assisted people all around the globe to benefit from a wide range of academic and professional studies free of charge.

Likewise, ignoring the pleasure of immediate gratification, Professor Yunus, devoted his prime years to 'studying poverty reduction' and initiated a seed project called Grameen Bank, a micro-finance lending scheme that alleviated the scourge of poverty among rural dwellers in Bangladesh. The scheme has grown by leaps and bounds and is now being copied by different institutions across the world in order to mitigate the fiery pressure of poverty.

Most successful individuals and enterprises pass through this path less-travelled by others, that is, the path of a unique service proposition embedded in sacrifice and focus for the future. And genuineness, an expression of one's value, breaks every wall of mental dullness and makes the extra journey worthwhile and fulfilling.

Leading can then be viewed as a drive along one's mission that opposes stagnation in the face of worthy adventures, but allows a cautionary behavioural-interphase when faced with a scary billow of oppositions, be they caused by people or from conditions, threatening one's dream/purpose.

Enrichment truly comes when we give of our time and resources for the benefit of others.

Part B

Fasten your Dream Belt

Chapter 4

A Flint in Time

To stay motivated is to stay alive.

From the cradle to the grave, in the infinite passage of time, everyone's history is recorded. But the reality is that some people make their histories or stories livelier than others and they do this by active engagement with their dreams. These, their dreams, get them turning over in top gear and, because of their dreams, they stay motivated.

Because there is no universal definition of the word 'motivation' and different theories of its meaning tend to be understood by different management students, we shall look at the concept by observing it in the lives of certain remarkable individuals, individuals who leveraged their inner treasures and derived meaning from smallness. These individuals showed 'courage' and 'determination' in living their dreams and were 'excited' about them. Assigning the CDE's of Motivation to everyday activities provides an essential guarantee for realising a worthwhile experience.

Let us consider The **CDE** in simple terms:

Motivation is deciding or signing with your mind
not to stop/daring to dream.

Courage is the strong face of determination employed in beating against the odds. A courageous person is not only determined to achieve his or her goals but always comes up with new ideas, schemes, ways or inventions to attain those goals.

Determination is drive and persistence in working for your dream, irrespective of your excitement state (whether the weather is favourable or not). Chasing after a dream is not easy for many of us. I have listened to lots of elderly people, and young ones as well, who say that they would have loved to chase their dreams but didn't because they felt unable to. They felt that taking such a path was scary.

Excitement is seeing your dreams come true or being passionate/certain that they will.

Motivation is like a spark that sets a dry forest on fire; it is like a tender root that draws us towards the oasis of fulfilment. In fulfilment of the end goal of mankind, that is, happiness – as is commonly agreed by billions of people – motivation plays a key role. It is the drive that sets your heart reeling for happiness when inspired by a dream. It asks, is this possible even if it seems impossible? And if it *is* possible, however remotely, then determination can be employed. If a goal is not achieved at the first attempt, motivation can drive you on another dream journey, a dream similar or in line with your original dream, and determination can help you to sail through the rough patches of troubled waters. Determination in this context means to never give up.

Like winning, motivation is not a one-term affair. 'Cowards die many times before their time', is a popular saying. But, to put it the other way round, winners live many times before they truly live. They keep dreaming. They dream many times and work on a number of dreams before their lights suddenly break forth as does the morning star, or as a rainbow that accompanies a heavy pouring of rain. That is why the geniuses who fill world-record books have usually undergone many trials. Winners keep dreaming and daring – until they find their seemingly impossible Eldorado.

Motivation is that little voice that keeps reminding you to believe in your worthy cause even if it is unheard of and/or seems unrealistic. Motivation tells us 'yes, it is possible' and it is a genuine quiet voice. Of course, if we listen to this little whisper and respond by acting with determination, we risk name-calling by those who do not believe in our dreams.

Whatever the outcome, history favours those who attempt their dreams with an open mind.

One dream that still lingers gigantically in the long tunnel of time stems from the identity-desire of one man, Christopher Columbus. No one can deny that he brought the Americas to limelight and memories of his achievement abound. As proof, there is the Washington District of *Columbia*, USA; British *Columbia*, Canada; the city of *Columbia*, South Carolina; and the country *Columbia*, among other locations named after him.

His dream remains fulfilled.

His primary *passion* was travelling. It became his *talent* as well as his *desire* and the oceans became his playground though many a times the tide-race roared. At the heart of his desire or dream lay another notable desire – to bring to his compatriots an epic message of new-found lands never before known by his people. This was his *value*. Since he believed that the labourer is worthy of his hire, he also desired recognition and asked to be *identified* as the "Great Admiral of the Ocean". This can be seen as his patent, his claim to ownership of the discovery. He, in addition, set a *system* in place to pay for his fleet by seeking support from the government of the day.

But then came hard knocks of fierce opposition from jesters and those who doubted his belief-system of over-arching dreams. He did not waver and, even in the face of physical *threats* and his own personal *failings*, he was *courageous* enough to skim towards the horizons of life, making certain of his achievement by making not just one trip across the Atlantic but by a couple of such. Then fortune shone for him.

In the race of life, it has been echoed abroad, only the brave are decorated by the goddess of fortune. Sensing their time, their mood and their destiny, the brave set forth with their mind as set in flint, on a desire, for a dream, and they are never stopped by the vicissitudes of life.

And also in our own time, Magic Johnson's aura reverberates and asserts that he was a man of passion and courage. He lived the dream of being a record maker/breaker – of one that would have his impact felt both within and beyond his immediate neighbourhood. His strong disposition towards his inner value was only spurred on after he encountered what others once referred to as his downfall.

After being given a death sentence, for so it was those days, a diagnosis of that then-little-known and scary condition called HIV, this victim or convict, not of civic litigation but of perception of death (for what frightens more than thought of death itself?), eventually resigned from his basketball team but, rather than dying, set his face as in a flint and overturned the sentence by keeping alive his dream for more than two decades – and still waxes stronger, bubbling in hope and offering life to those scourged by society.

A member of the 1992 Olympic dream team and with numerous awards from the NBA, he reverted to his earlier goal of being a business man who could influence public opinion, influencing it not through commentary of words but by flying actions, the actions required to transform a particular type of community, a community often overlooked by businessmen – the minority neighbourhoods of the inner-city urban areas.

He pioneered the establishment of mega companies in these neighbourhoods and even approached the world's largest coffee house, Starbucks, and Starbuck's CEO, Howard Schultz, was quick to relate to Magic Johnson's dream and remembered his own 'escape' from his own socio-economic struggles, in Schultz's case, through 'dreaming' of making coffee in a café into a communal experience, and thus Magic Johnson achieved his goal but not by the route of sport, as he once experienced it.

Coupled with his *value* and the lessons learned from a system that supported his basketball talent, Johnson courageously opines that, when folks entrust their brands in partnership or franchise to you, it is like your team mates passing the B-ball to your hand; they do it because you get them a point. His drive and focus was carried over from his basketball dunking skills, empowering him to look within and reassert his dream of becoming a symbol for society. With this in mind, his business acumen became matchless and his success a phenomenon.

Anyone who has risen from low to high will assent to that old saying, "the end of a man is not in his downfall". A man dies when he stops dreaming, even if he lives to be another Methuselah.

Certainly, this generation will also not forget Samantha Bailey. Among those who walk the path of their dreams, she will rate high. Listening to her story, I knew that, as compared to others with similar stories of waiting for a talent show, she was motivated by a genuine, burning desire and not simply by a talent for showing off. Long before her final contest in the British X Factor, I had pencilled her in for the topmost prize just as many others must have done, despite discounting for any bias that the world may have for younger talents, who also were among top contenders in the tenth series of the competition.

She followed her passion, though the world might say that she had waited long. I felt that she had mastery, even if unknown to her, of the power of the unwavering little voice of light, the little voice of light which many call 'constancy of purpose' or 'desire'. Leaving her comfort zone, her work as a prison officer, and having nursed her dream for twenty years, she became an overnight international music sensation. Her tenacity was well displayed in her work-out rehearsals.

The framework of this book will not allow us to draw an analogy with the glowing praises given to others such as Ray Kroc, whose overriding madness for cleanliness catapulted McDonald's into becoming a world-renowned eatery, or of Walt Disney or Steve Jobs, among those that soared to great heights on the wings of their particular passions.

These examples demonstrate the essential virtue of staying strong (motivated) with your dream(s).

Consider, how lasting will your own impact be on the face of time when you connect with your mind and actualise your dreams?

Imagine what excitement you will bring to somebody else.

In summary, a working *system* recognises and, often times, appreciates *talents/innovations/ideas*.

- Though interchangeably used, p*assion* and *desire* are driven by *values*. You can have both *passion* and *talent* or either.

- Our *identities* are our impact/significance or end results.

- A gap exists between *threats/failings,* and *courage*.

Chapter 5

The Beauty Beneath

When we 'really' appreciate what we've got, which is our mind and our time – life and how we spend time with the other, our people – then our value appreciates.

The wind of change blows and it threads through the work we do. Whether working smarter or harder, work is still work. To try to conquer the world without conquering oneself is an exercise in futility. At the end of the race, it is only those that have competed with honour that are rewarded. Champions who cut corners yesterday are today stripped of their trophies by the court of time and, except in exceptional circumstances, history has little respect for those who do not complete their race at all. Many knowingly or unknowingly start in a race that they cannot complete, and many are still in the valleys of decision as to which race they should enter. A journey of a thousand miles may begin with a small physical step but it can only be completed through the potency of the traveller's mind.

The mind is like the open field which, when left in idleness, degenerates and produces weed but, when obliged to make an effort it, gets renewed and when cultivated and nurtured it will yield great abundance. The mind is like an ocean bed covered with the daily streaming of tidal waters which, when awakened, gushes oil. It is like the fruitful earth; the surface soil does not usually produce diamonds and gold not unless a pickaxe or a digger is applied. If this is true, the beauty of the soil often lies in its discomfort and, likewise, the mind also must be stretched.

Do you have dreams of how your life might be? If you only know the easiest thing to do, then you are a step further from living them, because the easiest thing, my friend, is to do nothing, the easiest thing is to do what you have always done, and the tough job is thinking through the right way to proceed. By thinking differently, you can act differently. If you knew Morris Goodman, the motivational doer, and how he recovered from a plane crash injury against medical explanation just by thinking in his mind of recovery, you will believe what Ghandi said: 'What he thinks, he becomes'. If we don't dig out our dreams like gold or diamonds, we end up despising the only true asset we have – our mind. Only time will tell if we succeed or fail.

Time and again, it has been said, the gods will not do for man what he ought to do for himself. The Parable of the Talents (Matthew 25: 14-30) describes this well; it comes from the Holy Book.

A man gave to each one of his servants, according to his ability, a bag of talents (money) and advised them, 'occupy yourselves till I come'. So it is with each one of us to whom all of life tells us 'move', for any seed remains a seed if its radicle does not exert itself. Life is only felt in motion. Even the heart of a prisoner moves, it beats, the blood, the very particles of life, move to and fro in the veins and the arteries. The mind, the seed wherein the germ of success is housed, needs to be stretched and guided in order for it to become a firm root. The mind should be moved in its essence towards light rather than through fear. If it does so then the body can be made to perform effectively through work. Learning to generate the right choice of a motivating idea can be the key that starts the journey, but you must also *move*.

When full moon returned, the master returned. Two of his three servants whom he found to be diligent were doubly promoted based on their performances. Each of them posted a 100% profit on the talent they had been given and, if 100% increment was realised, perhaps 100% commitment to dream development can be inferred. However, the last partner was punished, not because he made a profit less than 100%, but because he neither traded with his talent nor kept it in the bank for interest; he just kept it as it was. The gift entrusted to his care was neither explored nor exploited.

That master is like life. The wicked servant believed that the master had been hard on him but he was judged from his own words, because his mind-set did not value the gift nor the giver nor the traders who could have benefitted from the merchandise. The sickness of man occurs when he follows a path of stagnation when faced with responsibility and challenges.

Better to be known as 'Mr or Ms Tried' than 'Mr or Ms Do Nothing.'

Our minds are akin to those servants. In due season or at various times, life demands of us that we move and act. Yes, it is true that sometimes the pressures of life can seem insurmountable, especially when a series of calamities suddenly strikes at a single stretch and, at such a time, doubts about these conditions can, arguably, be pardoned. However, unpardonable with regards to success, or rather, with regards to failure, is the soul in full capacity that yet decides to do nothing and champions the notion that 'life is not fair'. Life does not respect any person because of how they 'feel'. A stone thrown against a strong tree is the same one that bounces back, and a person's perception – how his/her mind interprets a sight – is to be blamed. Wrong perception, and only that, can lead you to do nothing to further your path in life and to claim instead that 'life is not fair'.

The servant who made no profit from his talent was punished. His talent was confiscated and handed to the man who had made the highest profit. And this parable is useful for us because – as the world finds hard to ignore – the rich keep getting richer and poor keep getting poorer. And also, those successful in one field obtain prizes in other heights if they choose to change their path. Success is therefore not merely the possession of ability, but the practice of *moving positively* with your ability.

If this parable were merely of historical interest or was

out of date and had not been tested in the hard school of the modern world – since everyday reality is not static – then it would be of no use. But it should be noted that the outcomes of numerous modern scientific investigations, as exposed by Peter Drucker, the widely acclaimed Management Guru, demonstrate that outstanding achievements, at least those at a level below the shattering achievements of great people such as Albert Einstein or Max Planck, are not simply dependent on ability but are also dependent on the sheer guts of those scientists who pursue their opportunities. George Washington once opined: the world cannot care less about how much knowledge you possess but only about what you do with it.

Truly, the good works of many, be they geniuses or otherwise, are never buried; they live after them and are a posthumous reward for the courage of those who did them. Against the odds, the Lady with the Lamp, Florence Nightingale, found her niche and performed dutifully. Her parents thought that the nursing profession was too inferior for someone of her social stratum to get involved in, but she reasoned with them and believed that nothing was too small if it were for the service and benefit of mankind – and, until the present day, the nursing profession pays her homage for the role she played in history, of caring and catering for the medical and sanitary needs of the people she looked after. And likewise, history remembers Mary Seacole who, though faced with racial prejudice and hindered by financial constraints, set her mind to venture forth on the right cause and risked her life to help wounded British military personnel during the Crimean War.

The key to being successful is to appreciate and trade with those ideas and passions that are uppermost of the priorities in your mind, to go with them, whether you are self-employed, about to be employed or already working for an organization. Start right; get trained by diligent minds in your chosen field.

Show me a success story and I will show you a person of skill. The outstanding technician, lawyer, artist, athlete, engineer, designer or worker is no other but one who skilfully delivers his or her impact in such an uncommon manner. By understanding the nitty-gritties of his or her work through learning, they wisely apply knowledge to their endeavours. Hence, the end product of learning is success. To move and win, learning has to be upgraded.

All who appreciate and value the treasure that they harbour will find themselves commended. Employers will be grateful to the individual who works along his/her purpose together with his/her employer, who stays put, not out of complacency but in order to build and move the company's brand to greater heights – because therein lies his/her own individual happiness. The story of EBay, for instance, would not be complete without acknowledgement of the impact of Margaret Whitman in transforming the organization to a global e-retail force, increasing the company's size from $86 million to $8 billion within a ten year period.

This worthy reference can also be accounted of others like Sir Terry Leahy, former CEO of Tescos, who, starting as an employee stacking shelves, rose from zero to hero in search of meaning at the company and eventually fronted a giant leap for his employer, thereby steering the company's fortune to become the largest grocery store of his time in the UK.

Rejected by many companies after graduation, he managed to find his way to Tesco after a brief period working for another organization. At a certain point in his career upwards, he was made a marketing director – but one with an empty office and no team to help him when crisis struck the consumer market. During this time as marketing director, this man from an average background discovered the most important thing of all: according to him, his gemstone was 'time to think'. He thought then moved and eventually revolutionised the industry with an IT-integrated loyalty scheme that competitors initially ridiculed, but later envied and copied.

Loyalty is not the only way. Gratitude follows those who discover that their purpose is not to be found with their employer and, however tempting the wages, decide to move on in pursuit of happiness, to sail uncharted waters by activating potential's paddle. In this case, Mo Ibrahim, a self-made billionaire and philanthropist, reasoned:

'What do you do if you're an executive who decides to resign? You declare yourself a consultant'.

And so it was for the man whose 'declared consultancy', commenced in the garage of his house and who occupied his time with noble deeds. His last employer was unable to think through or visualize his dream, so this man leapt on the rope that has conveyed other achievers among mankind, the 'do-it-yourself' rope. His mind was moved and his body and his life followed.

Balanced against the risk and uncertainty of a new venture, he saw, just as in the seemingly unending waters of the Amazon, the unending match of seller and buyer that the e-commerce world could offer. This rope, the do-it-yourself philosophy, whose anchor point lay in learning about the industry he intended to enter into, was his starting place of opportunity and action, his walking place – because he walked the walk of success. A decade ago, I referred to this, and till now, Jeff Bezos keeps dreaming and his firm's fortunes rank among Forbe's global ten most innovative companies of year 2013.

A sickening condition, but worth mentioning, is that of people who chase other's passions but not their own. Perhaps such people will keep on living, but they will never fully live up to their potential until they realise what it is that they truly desire and chase after it. A potential/ dream/vision is but a promise and, as such, is only a debt – until focused dedication to duty to one's own purpose is applied and delivered. Zig Ziglar affirms: 'You are the only person on earth who can use your ability. It is an awesome responsibility'.

Live up to your responsibility. Your world is counting on you to do a noble deed today, be it as a cleaner or an astronaut, no matter how small or how big. Who knows, you may be the next person to achieve 'Hoover' status in our time. To succeed in this, you need to walk and work according to the pace of your ability and not that of others. Only then will you see the fastest of others as your breaking point as presented by Roger Bannister, when he broke the time limit on the four-minute mile – although your slowness will be your strength in the long run, as numerous geniuses in the arts, science and industry have shown. Go your fastest; no one with given ability should however crawl when they ought to run.

The beauty beneath the dream is thus best demonstrated in doing the right thing promptly – by moving with the mind first to deal with those issues that hinder your purpose in the world, through timely performance. The perfect time to start will never arrive. Perhaps there is a right time and it will surface but, for those no longer at ease, the time is now. I leave you with words of one of my favourite doers, Winston Churchill:

> *"To every man there comes in his lifetime that special moment when he is figuratively tapped on the shoulder and offered a chance to do a very special thing, unique to him and fitted to his talents. What a tragedy if that moment finds him unprepared or unqualified for the work which would be his finest hour"?*

Part C

Living Lights

Chapter 6

A Charter for Freedom

*The key to happiness is often times found
in redefining the key itself.*

Are we really happy or are we the prisoners of the processed thoughts, values and belief systems programmed into us over the years? Undoubtedly, some have understood that this can be so and have broken away from those 'perfect' societal assumptions as to what is considered normal. For instance, pursuit of career excellence by women was, in many societies, once considered an anomaly and those who rebelled against the *status quo* were tagged, 'rebels' or 'career women' by their communities. Owing to the courage of the pioneers, the impact of their life choices is felt in every sphere of life today.

However, when making such choices, it is necessary to assess the relevance of any particular expression of a fundamental human right. In many quarters, the choice for freedom has always been: 'to belong or not to belong'. For many men and women, the pursuit of goals such as career excellence brings with it a cloud that hangs over them and this cloud is a function of societal pressure, the pressure of the assumptions generally accepted by their society. This pressure, ironically, can be felt more in a crisis period. When called upon to oppose either employers or governments, some people simply go with the crowd whatever that may be. A striking example was the 2011 English summer of riots. An expression of anger towards the government was hijacked and degenerated into wild infernos across a number of counties. When the flames were washed off the faces of the protesters (mostly unemployed youths) in the courts of justice, some confessed that they opted for the action simply because it was the normal thing to do as confirmed by the fact that others of their friends were seen looting and destroying properties.

There is a natural tendency to cast aspersions on these young ones, some of whom felt neglected by the social system in place around them, but, in reality, flowing with the flow has become the in-thing for our society especially among the young who desire to conform and, on top of that, few will care about the relevance of your mission to society, be you young or old, if you are not yet in a social circle. In which case, they have no way forward, in the circumstances they find themselves in, except by conforming – or so they believe.

Something resembling this dilemma can be discerned in the life of young Charles Dickens. Unarguably, such an attitude as was displayed by the young rioters could have been a major contributing factor for the future author of *Oliver Twist*, who had no clear direction for himself in his early years and could easily have made wrong choices. He was almost torn apart by the social fabric of economic deprivation. Luckily, he knew that he wanted something more from life – he wanted to be famous. His propensity to stand against societal acceptance of wide economic inequality shines through his writings and edged him an advantage.

That was in the Nineteenth Century; the same can still be observed in this Twenty-First century of ours. There are different social classes but you can easily know where society fits you in when the parameters are checked. Broadly, there are: the upper echelons, the middle class and the lower-class.

To be of an impact, the societal torrent of the times demanded a lady who would enrol in a medical school or become a lawyer. Dancing to tunes extraneous to her, Chimanmanda Adichie fitted in and devoted her time to studying medicine. But had she not eventually listened to the rhythm of her heart and moved to the melody of her mind-changing course to learn to master writing, a profession considered by many in her country of birth as suitable for those who have chosen pauperism as a way for the future (except when rescued by dint of luck), perhaps she would have had no impact, let alone the fame and fortune that life eventually gave her.

Chimanmanda Adichie became a famous writer with several internationally-recognised titles to her name, and she was the 2007 Orange Broadband Prize Winner for Fiction. She was indeed rescued by both luck and hard work. As Publius Terentius once stated, 'fortune favours the brave', and so, also, many others have been favoured, who have ascended to new careers with a new lease of life, and all of them also refused to be limited by societal definitions of their talents, of who they are or who they ought to be.

The story of Chimanmanda Adichie is of someone from the upper middle class who moved to stardom, but the old adage reaffirms itself, 'what is good for the goose is good for the gander'; whether male or female, a star lies dormant in each one of us. And this could exactly be said of this remarkable woman who noticed her little light of writing since her infancy, but of whom societal pressure, even on the bridge of breaking forth to spring, demanded that she had better find a day job as an honest adviser rather than follow her understanding of who she was and where her passion lay. But if in the philosophy of mankind, a beggar – a socially deprived person – has no choice – although a beggar who 'may as well' and dares will know no bounds

At one time and from a societal perspective, J. K. Rowling identified herself as a failure. She was jobless, on the welfare-benefit system and diagnosed with depression, but, on discovering where she truly belonged, a place of her own, her light shone through the darkest night until the arrival of her day-star. Despised and rejected by many as being incapable of catching hold of fame, her writings at last brought sunshine to her world. Harry Porter became a household name and Joanne Rowling smiled at the banks, one of only a handful of well-revered money-machine authors and one of the richest people the world has ever produced.

On a related topic, on the need to assess one's relevance to others, it should be remembered that access to education, that force for freedom and change, should be the right of all.

However, to suggest that not everyone needs to enrol at a university may incur criticism – even though evidence abounds that this can be so, evidence of captains of industries who were college drop-outs and were once considered social eccentrics, people such as Sir Richard Branson of the Virgin Group, and Rosalia Mera of Zara Fashion House among others.

One's stance, whether to conform or not to conform, remains the trigger for societal acceptance or rejection. Society sets the standards as to what things to do, when they should be done, how they should be done, and with whom to do them. In some instances, such as seen in the case of ex-convicts despite the prison institutions have attempted to impart skills for living, the expectations of society usually result in ex-convicts doing nothing.

These conformist standards, though aspiring to, or apparently helping to, transform individuals into complete beings, create apathetically-equipped citizens who have a high dosage of fear of rejection by society, to the extent that innovation is continuously crippled and people stay on the verge of creativity, not knowing whether they are here or there, and the relevance of formal education is in doubt and distorted in its application by the wavering mind.

Societal standards, for checks and balances, are needed, they are essential in prevention of crimes and in stopping the worst learning-outcome deformities. If there were no checks and balances in place, deformities of the mind would become rampant and more men would continue as boys and not assume responsibilities nor learn to change when circumstances make this necessary, for instance when change is demanded by new trends in technology, style and design. And standards change also. If had not been for the new standards that emerged afterwards, the horrendous impact of Thalidomide in 1960s would have continued in multiple human deformities caused by continued use of the drug. Before the disaster, the world believed all medicines were beneficial. In other words, not all potentials or talents are beneficial if not properly fine-tuned and at this juncture, the societal relevance of standards and how they are set plays a pivot role in ethical decency.

But it is unethical for society to confine anyone to a social prison of irrelevance owing to their social status, birth deformities or physical impairment, especially in the case of birth and physical deformities, as can be seen in many developing countries where the disabled are neither provided with social benefits nor with easier access to employment (all justified by the notion that this neglect serves to foster their personal masteries and independence), but are subjected by societal opinions to a life of penury and alms sourcing.

Nonetheless, the art and ability to overcome disability is demonstrated by many people who live with difficult physical conditions but refuse to be socially curtailed from dancing to the beats of life (a passion unwrapped by a productive system). Tom Yendell, as an example, was a victim of Thalidomide but uses his other body parts in lieu of hands to produce wonderful art and design. With over five hundred works of art to his credit, this artist of global repute has some of his works printed on cards and wallpapers.

To take another example, Huang Guofu of China refused to be mentally bound and ventured into the production of art by painting with his mouth. His case is particularly significant because he chose to be competitive in his profession and not to be pitied. When he learned that most of his admirers purchased his works out of sympathy but complained about the quality, he fine-tuned his art and used his paint brush with the aid of his teeth rather than his feet – and has become a force to be reckoned with in the world of art.

A sweet fragrance in history also, is the legacy of Helen

Keller, the famous political activist, who was an advocate for people with physical disabilities and brought their plight before the relevant authorities. Also, Louis Braille, who invented the Braille System which has made formal education readily accessible and convenient for the blind. Both Helen Keller and Louis Braille were blind, but they lighted their world for others to see the beauty of revolutionary engagement despite society's perception of them.

Sometimes it is difficult to ascertain whether a disability caused a choice for destiny to be made or whether this was for some other reason. For instance, Warren Bennis was a lecturer who developed ideas about leadership as a field of human endeavour, but he rose to greater prominence by venturing all his talents and passion in a different channel – but only after suffering a biological set back. Why is our best often revealed at our lowest ebb, when obstacles raise their head to block our way as the rock of Gibraltar, long after we have hardened our hearts against listening to those inner yearnings that press us for expression. The answer lies in the old saying: 'he that is down needs fear no fall' – provided he chooses to move his mind. If he does not move his mind, he may stay perpetually down.

On a similar note, along with all the geniuses already mentioned and true to the words of John Mason, 'every obstacle presents a man to himself', Yinka Ayefele should also be remembered. Soliciting money from the public, he could only raise a small sum of money to finance medical surgery abroad, after he had suffered a ghastly auto accident. His condition was deteriorating but then a friend suggested that he try music. The problem was that he was an unknown musician and he was at his lowest point.

To be fair, his performances were already well admired by his countrymen but only in series of musical interludes. He was actually an employee of a national radio broadcasting station but his flames of passion had been extinguished by societal demands, his parents had rejected music as a profession for him. He had been a gracious chorister at his church from an early age which attested to his musical ability, but he had programmed his mind to want to become a banker, a clerk or, as he found himself, a radio presenter.

By listening and acting according to his passion, he switched on his musical prowess and was able to raise enough money. He underwent surgery abroad and founded a melody kingdom. Hoping one day to fully recover from the spinal-cord injury he had suffered, he continues to give a smile to millions across West Africa via his shining armour of strength, of singing. He also employs an appreciable number of employees.

This needs to be reiterated. Except in the case of folks with mental impairment, there is no limitation to the potency of the mind. History is rich with cases of former prisoners, such as Nelson Mandela, who have become presidents; on the other hand, a man who fails to recognise his inner light is a prisoner of self. A man or woman, able or physically challenged, who, according to societal standards, is regarded as free but who burrows in the prison wall of self-limitation owing to his/her obedience to society's perception of his/her abilities. Such a man/woman is indeed disabled.

A charter for freedom hence entails a choice that only you can make as to what you like doing that is beneficial for you and can be of benefit to your community – in the long-term, even though such a choice may initially be disregarded by those around you. There is a tale to tell: a treasury-art-island to design and a cluster of other opportunities that only you can realise.

Remember a popular game has always been to ask, 'what can you do if you were handed a $000'000 cash gift to actualise your dreams?,' but a greater question, as once aired by an inspirational teacher, is 'what can you do if you know you are at the lowest ebb of your life and everything else depends on you alone?' Why don't you consider this – regardless of pressures yet unknown? Don't let anyone except, in the case of fine tuning, define the choice for you. Only you have the key that can determine your long-term happiness! Explore your talents and passions!! Be free to be you!!!

Chapter 7

A Bird of Light

Passion is to life what oxygen is to fire;
passion is fuelling up choices to life.

Why are certain species of beetles called fireflies when not all of them emit light? This is why I prefer birds to fireflies because only on rare occasions would any bird not utter a sound to showcase itself. There is more to this than meets the eyes: "Petit à petit l'oiseau fait son nid" – 'little by little, a bird makes its nest'. The daunting task of nest-making may seem insignificant in the light of human passion, in this instance, the enthusiasm needed to make a nest. Small but tenacious, birds make of their lack of strength a mere triviality and pursue, little by little, their goal, their nest. They are passionate about meeting their potential in building a home for themselves though they have but little physical strength.

From a negative emotional outburst associated with

childhood bullying, we have seen how passion can be turned into productivity through perseverance. For instance Tendulkar, the world's most reputable Indian cricketer, had a childhood passion and this was rechanneled positively, and built on, through enrolment in the school of perseverance and with the support system of his family and mentors. There was also Demosthenes of ancient times, who, though disadvantaged by a speech impediment, devoted his time and with infinite patience mastered the art of public speaking in and out of season, and therewith, became the orators' orator.

And yes, there was another former stutterer by the name of Jack Welch of General Electric who, unlike other competitors for high position, lacked support from senior colleagues, but spoke up for himself. When asked by his predecessor, 'on whose head does the cap fit who can direct the affairs of the company', this well-revered, charismatic manager replied without hesitation, 'I'm the guy' and thus, as Wall Street legends tell, a leader was replaced with a live wire at General Electric. Jack Welch later became globally acclaimed as the 'Manager of the Century'.

A little strength with a bigger passion can scale a mountain especially when passion is wrapped with patience and focus.

There can be passion with little or no strength, but such strength can be built – and has to be built consistently in order to maintain stamina for the goal-building process.

It can be argued, why would the birds not sing when they are free to 'roam about' in the air? The answer is that, generally, they are known to be passionate creatures as metaphorically described by Maya Angelou in *I Know Why Caged Birds Sing*. While they tarry at work un-caged, they concurrently embrace their little strength as they intermittently perfect their talents and, perhaps, tell themselves to keep up the good work efficiently – as can be seen and heard, when they whistle and hustle, chirping and singing as they build.

Edison nailed it right when he said, 'all things become his who *hustles while* tarrying.' To win is to adopt a positive mentality (whistling) while channelling passion (hustling) for a worthy cause. It is sensible to say that no one can possess all things, but all things can be his who has peace. And peace is what is needed when passion has been positively channelled but yields no quick returns – a reassuring peace of mind that arises from knowing that nothing of great value comes easily except when a miracle of grace is involved. It is written in the book of history that many are saved by grace that results from this peaceful state of mind, achieved after engagement and passionate involvement, because, eventually, grace shines brightly on the man whose mind is full of light and joyfully revels in his duty as that of a burden of light though long it may be. This mystery can often be seen unfolding as in the works and lives of those that paint our world.

Through thick and thin, through war, revolution and famine, the painted treasure of Mona Lisa smiling gives gracious evidence of the painstaking effort undertaken by Leonardo Da Vinci while pursuing his purpose of beauty, and this painting also demonstrates how it also dispelled his many lone, lost seasons of artistic darkness. Louis Eilshemius could by any standard be regarded as a man of many colours, but a series of challenges through the decades forced him to an untimely resignation of his pursuit – just when his works were about to be appreciated. Vincent Van Gogh also, produced many works of art but sold just one. Though talented, his passion was smeared with anxiety and, in his toil, he suffered severe panic syndromes until death suddenly came along. The only painting sold in his lifetime, it is generally noted, was one that emerged when he was more at peace with himself than was usually his state of being.

'It is not work that kills a man', Beecher notes, 'but worry.' Cemeteries provide examples, through history, of the many successful people whose daylight turned dark owing to the evil hand of suicide. Alexis Carrol, a Nobel Prize Winner in Medicine put it another way, 'business men who do not know how to fight worry die young'. Passion should not ebb and flow if we are to make the best of it, irregularity should be challenged so that we can make a meaningful impact – and all this can be achieved through the mind being at peace with itself.

A cheerful mind-set is necessary, and not only at trying times but all the time. It is important to identify what gives you that shot of peace and tranquillity. If by walking around or praying during stressful times you obtain peace and quiet, by all means do so; and if it takes travelling across the sea to do the magic, don't hesitate to embark. By walking, journeying, moving or acting in any direction that encourages creative thinking and reflection, new ideas will flow into the mind. But if the mind, rather than beaming with peace and weighing the options, becomes fixed on the idea, the closed option, of travelling illegally across the sea for greener pastures but only as a route of escape, then danger looms. The key to misery is to be found in the waters of unbridled passion.

On the Island of Lampedusa and along the borders of the USA and Mexico, the most poignant examples of unguided passion unleash themselves in a myriad of disasters. By choosing to save themselves from poverty in their own countries, (not referring to those seeking asylum from war) many have lost their lives through illegal voyages, because their minds were negatively fixed – a case of passion directed but wrongfully guided, the mark of desperation, despair and despondency. 'When there is a will, there is a way', they say – but most of the reliable ways known to mankind are borne on the altars of wisely-guided will.

And yet, passion is to life what oxygen is to fire. Passion is the spirit of life. Lasting innovations, as we have already observed, run on the wheel of passion. Without a sufficient dose of passion, it will be difficult for you to adapt to the rapidly changing complexities of consumer taste, to changes in consumer demand, or to see and search out other opportunities that may arise from such changes, however highly skilled or talented you may be. If not passion, what was it that what could have made the two Michelin brothers scatter nails on the ground in order to demonstrate how small a thing can be the consequences of a flat tyre? They did it in order to demonstrate the application of the detachable, pneumatic tyre, and they later developed the radial tyre, whose variants are those found everywhere in today's market.

It was passion and they were sharp enough, early enough, to foresee and anticipate the many potential industrial applications of rubber when adequately processed thanks to the wonders of the recent invention of vulcanisation. Travelling on such tyres is now a major part of our everyday experience, but, before they came along, travelling on wheels was subject to a multitude of obstacles or inconveniences. For the brothers, 'the journey is the reward', as Peter Senge reflects.

'Nunc est bibendum' – 'It is time to drink obstacles,' said Horace. Fuelled by a passion that slaughtered obstacles and through hard work and sweat, the Michelin brothers were driven to make Éclairs, the first auto to ever 'run on air', thus culminating in Michelin's motto formation *Bibendum*. They were so driven by passion that a passionate guide – the Michelin Red Guide, was published with a debut record print run of about 35,000 copies, and this at a time when only between 600 to 3,500 cars roamed the streets and roads of France. The Guide catered to users of cars and to those who were considering it, guiding them to smile as they envisaged

their journeys of miles, thus confirming the doctrine of Thomas Edison mentioned earlier.

But life, like fire, is not just a triune component of body, soul and spirit, but in addition it involves complex reactions with environmental factors. And just as fire can be meaningfully directed to warmth by the right amount of air blown in the right direction, so also can passion be directed. Passion is of more consequence when it is reacting with the environment, particularly when it's challenged.

The eagle, that king among birds, is guided by a sense of restraint and, in its full passion and agility, closes its nictitating membrane so as to defy the heat of the sun. Perhaps, this sensing ability of the eagle that separates them from less common species, provides an analogy for the refusal for those passionate and talented captives, when it is required of them, in a strange land, to sing as in Psalm 137 as orchestrated by the Boney M's group, in the popular 1978 UK-No-1 single *By the Rivers of Babylon*. Not that eagles can't sing forever as caged birds do, but they predicate their actions on immediate environmental sensing.

Why would the captive in Babylon sing where they were despised? Because, when purposes are despised and abuse becomes inevitable, passion can stand up to the challenge, just as Christ drove out the temple traders because he knew that the place they traded in was meant for prayers. And it was passion that ignited both Édouard and André Michelin against malign opposition when their generosity was disregarded and, while their passion-born Guide was used to prop up a tyre merchant's workbench, thus inducing a reassessment of their approach.

Some things such as air, may be free, yet a free lunch rarely lasts and a price can be tagged on treasures.

Nonetheless, passion is priceless and can enable us to see where, and what, others despise and use this knowledge as a steppingstone to great achievement. For the eagle sitting alone on the mountain top sees in the landscape where its bounty lies. The opportunity for expression of passion is oftentimes within reach in our environment if it can only be sensed. And at a time when other operators scrambled to buy licences at great cost everywhere apart from Africa, the eagle-sense of Mo Ibrahim, originally from Sudan, made him turn to Africa for strength, and he created the world's fastest-growing mobile-phone market, launching it on a fire-selling spree across the only continent where licensing was free. Today, the international markets no longer talk of Silicon Africa as mere fantasy.

But even among the birds, including even the eagles, there are the birds of light that are more dignified in passion, particularly arctic terns. Though not as strong as the eagle, they possess a sensing strength typical of them. Irrespective of their colouration, they show strength in guided passion as they bask in the dawn of the morning, attuning themselves with the sun more than any other known bird and they migrate across continents, displaying a delight for summer lights and a disdain for winter darkness, and, by doing so, they live long and travel further annually than any other animal species.

As earlier stated, talent/strength, a platform for expression and a workable system all need to accompany passion in order for passion to be effective. When you are passionate for a fruitful outcome but with little strength or talent, skill must be painstaking acquired – as did the Wright Brothers before successfully piloting their plane that made them fly.

When a system or platform is absent, such skills should be created or searched for. It is not helpful to attribute our incapacity to generate workable alternatives to our religion or to use faith to justify the failure, for Jesus himself told us to be wise as serpents and withdrew Himself from various places of danger when confronted by wicked forces, before His purpose was fully accomplished.

And knowledge abounds of men and women of flesh, who like the bird of light seek options in order to actualise their life objectives (options not for the cause but for how to effect the cause) and thereby have generated value even when faced with systems unconducive to their missions.

One of such was Marie Curie, who created opportunities by searching and moving towards her goal. It was said of her that she was a woman possessed with a fever for hard work. Having decided that one Master's degree was not enough, she obtained two, one in physics and the other in mathematics. Marie Curie, born in the Nineteenth Century, was one of the most distinguished personalities the world has ever discovered. Born in Poland, she left her native country for France in 1891, aged twenty-four and full of ambition, in order to further her studies, because her country's university, the University of Warsaw, was not open to women.

Being courageous and hardworking, Marie became the first woman to win the Nobel Prize of Physics (1903, with two colleagues) and, later, single-handedly won the Prize for Chemistry (1911), making her the first to have ever won the

Prize twice in the sciences. Without this wonderful woman with her indomitable conquering spirit, less would have become known about the treatment of Cancer.

Passion, as noted above, can be reinvented in productivity by any system that favours the creativity of a sound mind. Such soundness of mind was demonstrated by Biju Thampy from Bombay who showcased light when everything around spelled doom and darkness. By Passion, Biju rose to the challenge of his time. Many had been aware of the poor street kids of Bombay whose sole priority was to survive, and he also, like others, almost ignored the noble call, however, on seeing a three-year-old kid drinking a dog's milk, he was overwhelmed by compassion. By an unplanned means, he showed light in the cosmopolitan city of Mumbai when the scary pressures of finance or lack of it and other logistical problems almost turned his mind from cleaving to a new vision of hope. He thus hoped 'to cater for just one street kid' and, although threatened by many difficulties, he committed himself and commenced his duty by feeding six kids.

At present, Biju, together with his team of Vision rescuers, has reintegrated many street kids into their families, restored focus among individuals and rehabilitated many young people from drugs and substance abuse. He has also rescued thousands who have been sexually trafficked, the sick, and children once blighted assumptions of societal inequality and injustice. A way will show forth, even in the darkest hour of the night, to those who take on themselves a burden, those filled with a warm temperament and a longing for worthy expression of their passion.

To sum up, passion entails defiance, embraces commitment and delights in the adventure of hope but may sometimes be hard to comprehend. This is demonstrated by the life of Paul Getty, once America's richest man, whose life revolved around a contrasting blend of passions, but who nevertheless focused on what he most desired, fanned his passions to life and realised his dreams. If passion is to life what oxygen is to fire, I suggest that we "keep the fire burning", fanning passion cautiously to life by focusing on the mysteries of treasures within.

Chapter 8

Colours and Seasons

Talents are treasure bearing seeds whose fruits though hanged
on systems are delivered by the stirring of values.

Short and simple, the poem below illustrates how we need to make constructive use of our resources.

A bell is no bell 'til you ring it,
A song is no song 'til you sing it,
And love in your heart
Wasn't put there to stay –
Love isn't love
'Til you give it away.

Oscar Hammerstein II

Augustus Weismann, a German biologist showed that when mice tails are cut off (unused) from the first to the fifth generation, the fifth generation still have tails. Through the generations, the tail-carrying genes remain. However, the mice whose tails were cut off may not have so much difference in beauty, seen as an aspect of utility, when compared to the last generation studied – if the last generation do not wag their tails.

With reference to the Parable of Talents (Chapter 5), recollect that the man whose talent (money) was withdrawn because he had not increased its value still had the capacity (skill) to trade, but his gift-beauty-trading profit-potential specifically from the money entrusted to him was cut off and given to someone else who could turn the talent to a thing of beauty. As you likely know, if we do not use our talents or capacities, regardless of their quality or power, such talents, ideas and dreams, though dormant, are often activated and expressed in various forms by someone else or even by robots.

There are many today who are gifted and multi-talented, as was Benjamin Constant, but who reject living to the height of their ideals and thus become void of strength in purpose and enterprise. Through his numerous artistic endowments and achievements, Constant the Inconstant, as Samuel Smiles described him in *Self Help*, died wretched after conditioning himself to under-utilise his potential almost as a matter of principle, and precisely when that was what mattered most. The world is more colourful today because, unlike Constant, numerous artists, writers and others such as Benjamin Franklin have lived life to the full and have been constant in purpose. These heroes wrote papers, crafted artworks, fought against slavery and are well remembered after death. Be reminded that you are crafted and designed for a purpose and that is the reason you are made for this season.

In modern times, where competition is stiff and a one-stop delivery phenomenon permeates every corner of society and of the market, it is important not to forget where you are and also the needs of the society around you. It is important not to forget who you are and what areas of your potential, mind-set and skills need development and, more importantly, where you are going – your aim based on a moral value. Do this in an honest manner and do not give in to *threats or belittling from others* who seem to be far ahead of you in your line of endeavour. They will not remain so if you stay true to your intentions.

To highlight how you should protect your product or talent from potential threats, management gurus of modern times refer to different managerial styles such as: Blue Ocean Strategy, Little's Law, Value Engineering, Low-Cost Strategy and Differentiation. If there is a view that is common to all these, it is that they want your product, service or talent to be different and differently positioned while you retain its usage value.

But even before these great management styles came to existence, Lars Ericsson did it his own way. Hardly is any time zone without smart phones in modern times, and the history of communication-convenience would not be complete without reference to the colossal impact of a telephone that Lars Ericsson designed. He, like numerous others, did not start from the top, but commenced his duties in the field he loved, telecommunications, and even though his was a little beginning – he was a phone repairer, and had his dream threatened by the American Bell Company which then dominated the market – he developed many managerial concepts unheard of in his time and manufactured a telecommunication instrument that was fit-for-purpose, light and attractive and which '*sharply differed from other telecommunication instruments of his time'*, with the intention that his invention should beat those of Bell and other rivals in the market when tested for simplicity, strength and splendour. Which it did. When you meet a need with a solution, it gets good; and when you upgrade the solution with your style, its colour or specificity comes more to life. Best things truly come in small packages.

Do what you love doing, as Chapter 6 suggests, but it is important that you eventually do what you love doing *your own way* and after having considered all contingencies, needs, purpose and trends. Some may say that you need to specialise, others that you should diversify, innovate, or brand your product or service or activity but, in a nutshell, *do it your way* is the mantra to use to guard you against anti-dream bullies. An adage makes it clear: 'the sky is wide enough for all birds to fly with their dreams'. The question is not simply about fine tuning your skills or doing what you like doing; it's about adding a positive emotional touch to what you aim to do.

Obtaining clues from many little things around you, as I have demonstrated, can thus facilitate your adherence to what the mantra says, *do it your way* – and this quest for *emotional* substance can be found *in all* fields of human endeavour where delight, purpose and a thirst for growth whether personal or financial or in any other form intermingle, and where daring to dream is the most important of all the things you can aspire to.

For instance Dolly Parton, the country-and-western singer, was well recognised for her musical talents from childhood. Being a particularly gifted soprano, she carved her niche. Venturing into country music, she became one of the ever-shining story-singing stars of her generation. It should nonetheless be remembered that the stories shared by her mum as well as the cloth of many colours crafted by her mum and given to her were some of the little things that Dolly transformed and drew on as inspirational drivers to attain what must have seemed to a child to be an unattainable height in music. Who could have thought that the diligent and painstaking work of embroidery and the 'mundane' story telling of her mother would one day be rewarded and heralded across the globe? Something good can arise from everything seen around.

It should therefore be no surprise that, while looking for talent, modern recruiters have relegated the traditional process of sieving through CVs and now seek to investigate a framework that looks for the little things that matter. Innovative employers have gone beyond the boundaries of conventional practice to search for those special things that differentiate an individual. This explains why big organizations such as United Parcel Service (UPS) or internet giants such as Google and Facebook rely heavily on big-data analytics (owing to its power in extracting and connecting little dots arising from a complex mix of volume, variety and velocity of all available information), to understand and project consumer demands and products. Indeed everything is everywhere – but the environment selects.

The environment also begets talent – what is the use of talent when it is not applicable to the society? Value or 'socio-economic profit' may be present in the production of goods but it can only arise from sales or market demand – from the social environment. In the same way, skills and capacity mean nothing when they are not in line with the needs of society. And though marketing, because it focuses on market needs, may generally be regarded as the cream of the crop for value-creation among business entities and organizations, it is the sellers' *attitude* that is more contagious, and his wits, proverbial and anticipatory, enable marketing to bear fruit. Playwright John Luther once said, 'natural intelligence, a wonderful education – none of these guarantees success; something else is needed – the sensitivity to understand what people want and the ability to give it to them'.

How did Ingvar Kamprad's IKEA dominate the furniture industry and obtain a higher performance in customer-loyalty rating than the industrial average even during the company's more critical moments? Even in 2010, a period characterised by reduced levels of consumer confidence in businesses and spending, the company operated beyond the caution of 'marketing myopia' and continuously sought to identify customers' needs so as to meet them. That this policy worked is evident from the (approximately) 626,000,000 visits by customers to company stores in 2010. The company is certainly not 'a complete whole', as is no other firm, but its culture of selling a 'lifestyle of good taste' is an intangible asset that has allowed it speedily to gain a reputation for dependability from its customers.

By making customers 'more partners than consumers', IKEA's financial policy of low pricing and self- assemblage of purchased products by customers became a source of strength and helped the company to increase its market presence across geographical borders. Altogether, the rare product strength of IKEA appeals 'in part' to the virtues ('needs' in Maslowe's terminology) of Esteem and Self Actualization found in the top-edge of hierarchy of human needs propagated by

Abraham Maslow. Although lacking in large funds of money, and contrary to popular opinion, middle-class and lower-class earners can 'buy' space and 'step up' to a sense of creativity, problem-solving, achievement and respect, while concurrently doing their bit to save the ecosystem through self-assembly of their bits of furniture.

Ingvar, like other such notable personalities, is known to have designed a personal philosophy for himself. He lived by it and managed to maintain an exemplary level of good conduct in his life of busy business engagement. IKEA is structured around his philosophy but the personal/emotional influence of it was balanced by dealing with the complex needs of society through a balance mix of marketing (sensing value need) and selling (delivering) stratagems.

While it is almost impossible for everyone to be an industrialist/brand manager like Ingvar Kamprad, it is important at least to be able to sell one's talent to the community, either freely or with a price, inasmuch as it serves a purpose and a need. These little things count.

Archaeologist, John Romer, and botanist, David Bellamy, co-authors of *The Seven Wonders of the World,* have contributed meaningfully to popular understanding of many aspects of natural issues. But, both know how to present what they love doing for the enjoyment of the public, and they feel out an audience when delivering talks on air. Scientific reporting of peat bogs and their excavation may be boring to most people, but these scientists deliver their work with tact and an understanding of the level of difficulty their audience can cope with.

Ben Feldman, acclaimed as the greatest life insurance salesman of all time, was known to be shy and spoke with a lisp, yet he rose to become the best of his kind and sold life insurance policies, in total, up to the face value of $1.5 billion. He made buyers see themselves as the people he saw in them – if they *used* his products, rather than if they merely bought them. He tailored his message to their level. His salesmanship was focused on 'smaller corporations' in Ohio and Pennsylvania and his career developed and multiplied even as these companies grew.

The ability to see and understand what others cannot easily see or understand in valuable resources, products or services, has most impact if such insights are initially tailored and sold to the dreamer by himself. Derek Powazek, for instance, the founder of Fray.com and a facilitator of numerous information-support systems, informed himself and empowered his own future by insightfully exploring his immediate environment. He discovered during his college days that he could access his school's darkroom free of charge if he joined the college newspaper club. Where others saw a newspaper club, he saw photojournalism and developed himself and his skill. By foresight, he conceived an idea that would one day change our social inclinations. His website is a true-life story-telling website that has unarguably contributed towards the foundation and proliferation of the two-way interactive-design mechanisms that have been used by blog webs and other social web pages.

Selling to oneself is akin to discovery, and 'discovery', Szent Gyorgi says, is 'seeing what everybody else sees but thinking what nobody thought'. A talented seller who delays and waits for perfect conditions in order to see clearly before starting may discover that he/she is left with nothing eventually. Even freelancing is a highly reputable option, and www.elance.com and other channels are there to enhance one's market visibility.

A good salesman deals with the business of life as if everything else in this world depends on his sales and not just his/her visibility and so tries to actualise any worthy deal or dreams as quickly as possible. David killed Goliath because he displayed a good salesmanship: 'believe in me, I have killed a lion and a bear recently, and I have got what it takes to make this season colourful for your kingdom', he pleaded with the King Saul so as to be allowed to fight the giant soldier.

However, 'as quick as possible' is subjective. A talented seller believes a 'no' can turn to a 'yes' with persistence but, also, that 'time waits for no one' as the saying goes. And if time does not wait for you, you should not therefore wait for time – except when your Creator demands it. You don't arrive by waiting; you arrive by moving, processing, sowing and selling (dreaming, propagating and cultivating) seeds of focus and purpose – perhaps on different platforms – hoping your seeds germinate quickly; but, on the other hand, you must remember that some dormant seeds, especially those of trees, pass through series of tests and take time to germinate. So, sometimes, waiting is what is best after all.

Abraham Lincoln's storyline of 'tests' to presidency typifies what inspirational leadership and freedom to dream entail. His opinion had always been, 'he would prepare and grab hold of opportunity once it presents itself'. We all know how many times he kept failing forward before the 'no-s' turned to 'yes' for him.

In 1980s, Tim Berners-Lee first conceptualised a global system based on a similar framework of the hypertext that could enable information-sharing among knowledge workers across the globe. It took 'a decade of time' before he became publically associated with the World Wide Web and before that time he had designed the first website in the world. He didn't simply attempt to tell a story in 1980; he continued to make the deal come true for a decade after. Like trees, both Lincoln and Berners-Lee laid the foundation for others to climb on and thrive.

It seems like, in all known history of great minds, it all starts with a story, an idea and a notion – but it is *the tenacity and the drive* through the seasons of tests and time that makes the difference between success and failure, severing the wheat (good ideas) from the weeds (ideas appearing to be good but are not), and this is what makes these great minds arrive colourfully with their dreams.

When the world passes comment at you for conceptualising a noble idea and all around seems like a chaos, keep working on those goals with your talents, and adopt a real seller's attitude. Ben Feldman observed, 'most people buy not because they believe, but because the sales person believes'. Believe and your dreams will be bought.

Chapter 9

To Dream Again

Each one is as rich as the substance of his dream and as poor as his fear.

In this dawn of the morning, it is easier for me, being seated and surrounded by beautiful books written by great minds, to forget the daily struggles of many in Africa, Eastern Europe and other parts of the world. I can choose to forget the pain and frustrations of the many street vendors in Accra or the water-pushing vendors of Shendam and of many others across various transnational cities and borders.

Oh! How can we not rejoice in the joy and transformation of one who, yearning and waiting, hoping the right day may arrive like a bolt from the blue, one day works the wonder of a sustainable livelihood.

To such a one who believes in the Infinite Being, and to those who don't, to those who never gave in to the whirlwind of extortion and other illegal means of circumventing the price of success, this prize is due. To the prodigal son also, who longs to return home after expending precious time and resources away because home is where the dream lies and where your treasure is and there, I say, *your heart will find peace*.

To the simple man or woman who cries and longs for a treasure from another land; to friends and lovers who, being filled with dreams and pride as kids, now see no glimmer of hope in the dark tunnel of life, filled with shadows of doubts and anxieties; to the young man, an orphan, who prayed he might relocate to a megacity if happily he could find fortune; to the hearing memory of the idle lips that wished to be in the place of a young executive not knowing the executive himself was pursuing a different dream; to many looking for a way of escape from job insecurity, underemployment, unemployment and false/forced employment; to the employee, employer and self-employed; to all such who dare to learn not to compromise on a worthy cause, I say, *hold on to life*.

Through struggles, rivalry or competition there remains the inevitable essence of life. Life should not be a rat race. Competing in the rat race may enable survival and satisfaction in the short term but it thwarts reinvention. For the long-term, those individuals that flourish with their dreams and look beyond the rat race find true innovation, be it of renewed processes, ideas or partnerships. These dreamers are those who do not see threats in those things that numerous others do.

These individuals do acknowledge threat from the down times of life but do not subscribe to them; they exploit them instead. Warren Buffet is a classic example of such a one and is representative of a group that finds its anchor in the economic cycle of life and has the strength and vision to invest during bust periods. Adrian Wooldridge's article in the *Economist* on Global Heroes (2009) shows that, downturns present an opportunity for renaissance for economic productivity. Prominent companies such as Gap, Microsoft, Polaroid and Hewlett and Packard among others, were born in the depths of depression and recession. Even, Net a Porter, the world's premier and most successful online fashion house, commenced trading activities during the dotcom bust era.

Therefore, never throw away that element of substance that you once held so dear in your heart but that has since been masked and torn by the challenges and darts of life. Acknowledge your given socio-economic boundaries but live beyond them. Raise the standard of your mind. Start to live again.

During critical moments, people often ask, 'how can I renew my dream or start to live again when I have nothing'? Another way of putting it might be: "yes, I am aware that everyone in a right-thinking capacity has something to offer his/her generation, but what impact would my little contribution make to people in my society, some of whom are also likely to reject my actions, talents and goals?"

Who could argue? I also agree that we, as a species, are more attracted to largeness, established trends or successful brands, rather than smallness or start-ups. Our common perception of, and affinity for, bigness is so strong that many believe that big corporate entities such as Enron Brothers, Lehman Brothers, Salomon Brothers or Northern Rock are too big to hit.

For a truth, rather than being afraid of larger-than-life personalities and entities or any other such dominant entities, it should be remembered that, according to James Bryant Conant, 'a turtle makes progress only when he sticks his neck out'. And to dream again, fear must give way to courage, fear of whatever kind, of being despised by friends or loved ones, of not knowing what length of time it will take to reach a goal, fear of the shame that accompanies a first or subsequent failure, fear of not having what it takes and, finally, fear of the unknown.

Kevin Rose, a Partner with Google Ventures can be regarded as an advocate in 'guts mapping = following your instinct'. Like many of us, he was initially scared of the big success stories in the tech industry but, on conquering the fear associated with starting a new firm, he founded Digg and subsequently several other companies. Kevin stated that there had been no threat to him in starting or continuing in his line of talent and passion – unlike what he initially feared.

Dreams do well with little capacity when fear is dispelled.

However, when his businesses were booming, the thought of the problems associated with business expansion niggled at him and he downplayed his strength. He reluctantly succumbed to fear in managing his much-coveted treasure. According to him, rather than participate and speed up by learning about practical business modules, he hired specialists to take charge of certain aspects of his business empire which he felt incompetent to handle, but by doing that he learned the hard way. He failed to adhere to the correct boundaries of delegation and authority, as laid out by Henri Fayol, the Management Guru.

Elbert Hubbard said, 'he who is out of problems is out of the game'. What did Kevin Rose do that we all have not done before? We all like to be competitive but we avoid problems by following what major competitors have already done. We also, most of us, have often delegated the boundaries of our dreams, hopes, ideas, prospects, opportunities and leanings to forces beyond our control, that consequently dictate their terms to us. When Natalie Massenet first dreamed of founding a chain of coffee shops, various specialists and advisers despised the idea and told her that there were no money to make in coffee making. Some months later, Starbucks hit the street and became an overnight phenomenon. She learned her lessons. When advisers promised doom and failure for her second dream, of online business, she would not be beaten twice. She despised the wisdom of the doom tellers.

Just as Kevin and Natalie later reasserted their authority and were able to dream again, most other individuals can be rescued from loss and shame if they have the will. Regardless of any losses we have suffered, we too can begin to work out those areas where our authority can be reasserted and then therefore dream again. But, to do this, it is important that some fundamental forces that we have relied on for survivorship be carefully considered.

Some significant strategic forces or socio-economic

models may seem to have lived up to our expectation of them in certain areas when well implemented, but several studies have also exposed a need to assess such models or strategies in the light of specific conditions. Rather than build on their own particular competitive strength or advantage, many have *diversified* their businesses unnecessarily or *initiated sales price slightly below or about* the same as those of market leaders, without considering their own cost of production nor what other values the market leaders offer for delivery.

What is being observed nowadays? A considerable proportion of businesses formed by new entrepreneurs do not survive in the long-term. A reliance on foreign direct investments, especially in developing countries, has enabled more companies to transfer funds and profit efficiently within themselves, rather than grow their profits by creating more job opportunities for the locals. The utopia of privatisation has lost its firm grip. To some, the revolutionary storm of new technology of recent times has blown along with it unemployment, underemployment and job insecurity. Given the above, it is of utmost importance that value champions confront these negative conditions with their 'mystery man'.

The 'mystery man' to which I refer is a little sprig of

hope on a pupil's chest that makes him believe that life is opened up by opportunity. As kids, countless numbers of people have envisioned themselves as the next architects of their world but, as life unfolds, what was once a fancy stares at them across the stark reality of time. George Orwell in *Why I Write* lamented the distribution of good fortune after observing that individuals lose their purposes and identities to the iron man of drudgery and servitude when reaching the age of about thirty.

Surely, in certain aspect of life such as child bearing, it matters when you deliver – the early bird, as they say, gets the worm – but when it comes to the race of life, each one of us must run according to his/her own time and purpose. Napoleon Hill, some decades ago, warned us of our need to abide by the pace or movement of the clock of our life and pointed out that a significant number of individuals start actualizing their long-term dream on or about the age of fifty. In recent times, the results of a study popularised by The Kauffman Foundation attest that the number of business proprietors over the age of fifty was double that of those under twenty-five in a ten year review of the business sector.

You can be young or old and still succeed.

Nonetheless, neither age nor work-experience is the yardstick for measuring assertion of purpose, though age and work-experience can augment it. Simply put: tarrying too long at one's duties does not equate with being fulfilled. There are many, who can be called rich, who dine with rulers and work lengthy hours but who yet find no well of satisfaction to draw from in their life pursuits. So also there are many (see the storyline of *The Poor of Bogota*) who tarry long at their employers' factories only to be paid meagre wages after a day's hard work, and find no certain meaning to life. The only place where consolation is to be found is among that number who, whether tarrying long or otherwise, find a delight in their job because it tallies with the causes of their lives, be it those causes that speak to their values, talents, visions or goals. This delight, as a spring in the valley of drudgery, often times turns to a fountain-flow of health because the merry heart does well and delight is like medicine.

Take the story of a young, trainee journalist in a little town somewhere and with little pay. He lived strictly on a monthly budget and did not walk with his wallet. He was so poor, he thought he could only feed himself. One wintry evening, he saw a man, a traveller who had been robbed, sitting on the floor, and, though covered with blankets by another passer-by, the man was shaken and begging for food because he had been without water or food for some time. Seeing this, the young journalist, driven with emotion, went to an eatery not five yards away to purchase some food for the destitute man – only to remember, as he was about to pay the cashier, that he had no cash on him. He humbly told the cashier about the man in the blanket and the cashier told her manager. The manager, unfortunately, in an assumed friendly manner, ridiculed him: 'you came here without cash, and you are telling junk stories. Can't we see for ourselves that the homeless man has not requested any help from us?' While the manager was speaking, the cashiers attended to ten orders from other customers.

The poor journalist was filled with shame but, just as he was about to turn away, he came to his senses and remembered that this particular company often bragged of the responsibility of corporate society in the big townships. He drew out his identity card, showing himself to be a journalist, and hinted that the manager's words would head for the dailies the next day. Hearing this, the manager soft pedalled and followed the journalist and brought in the destitute for a meal. Thus, a trainee journalist became a policeman of moral and social consciousness.

All you have may be something that others call nothing, but you can dream and you can help your world with it.

To shed a little light on this story: money, definitely, keeps the world moving around and a good profit is appropriate for a labourer's contribution, but, in the long run, it is not just about the money but about the legacies left. Current socio-economic levers of power and the moral condition of the world have made a large mass of people live in fear and they concentrate only on possessing what can last them merely a life time. As such creatures of fear, they choose to live without incorporating their dream to their daily activities or work – and suffer thereby.

More generally, apart from the above interpretation of this story of the young journalist, it should be emphasised that, instead of addressing market specificities/forces and developing competitive muscles or talents for value creation, many business entities and individuals who started off with noble dreams later lose their way and tilt their attention mainly towards *being competitive* (surviving) rather than *beating the competition* (dreaming). In business circles, pricing (especially low pricing as earlier stated) and adversarial advertisements often serve the trend of survivorship.

This is not to suggest that adoption of low-penetrative pricing or any other such policy is necessarily bad for businesses, nor does it imply that businesses should necessarily not follow the leader (market leader or team leader). Rather the more general point is that instead of focusing on staying competitive, it is better to reinforce and deepen one's allegiance to the common value, worth, or purpose that a leader is committed to, and thus create a platform of expression for oneself and that can be of benefit to others also.

In the golden era of mass marketing, Hans Wilsdorf understood the trend of his time and industry and started his business dream by following the phenomenon of the mass market. He flowed with the competition by selling speciality travelling watches on a large-scale basis. He also became a force to be reckoned with among those who worked on the movement-mechanism of watches. Since the Sixteenth Century, the accuracy and movement-mechanism of clocks, especially pocket watches, saw rapid improvement by different market leaders yet the technical dynamics were far from perfection. The tools used were susceptible to dust and other weather-like conditions. Hans Wilsdorf's dream was to overcome these problems.

Hans and his team worked hard to establish themselves in this line in the early Twentieth Century, and they had another card up their sleeves. As if the prevailing conditions of the previous four hundred years were not enough by way of a problem, Hans took upon himself that, from the very start, he would overcome another challenge or problem – that of the replacement of large pocket watches with small watches to be worn by men as the norm. A change requiring wider societal acceptance. His objective was roundly ridiculed by other watchmakers of that time. Wristwatches were not then considered properly masculine and watchmakers across the globe were sceptical of this naive new value champion.

Hans, however, presided over the popularisation of wrist watches. He achieved accuracy of movement for small watches, and the small, delicate mechanisms of the watches withstood the colossal problems of dust-like conditions of manufacture and other such matters used to bolster the boisterous criticisms of the scorners. He worked tremendously on making the industry's standard his dream and on making his dream, the industry's standard, by fulfilling both a gap in the market and his personal ambition concurrently.

But then, another dream was added to his pipeline of

problems – he looked towards producing watches that would make glamorous souvenirs for attaining milestones in life pursuits, watches that could unwind by themselves over long periods of time. After many years of rigorous experimentation, Rolex-Oyster and Rolex-Perpetual wrist watches were manufactured and became the industry's landmarks. Today, each time Rolex is mentioned, it speaks of personal mastery or of being above the competition – rather than just being competitive.

Volumes could be written of Hans Wilsdorf the dream carrier, but let us focus on the following. Having little financial means when he started out, Hans, like a number of other business founders such as Ericson, Nike (Phil Knight), and Domino Pizza (Tom Monaghan) needed financial help in form of a partnership, or borrowed funds from others such as relatives (sister) or investors (brother-in-law) to realise his goals.

Hans's business's brand name came to be associated with nothing in the literal sense, but in reality it stood for 'prestige and pride'. To establish this brand name, he drew lessons – from experience gained on his career path – of notable brands such as Kodak, which also means nothing in the literal sense but means 'defining moments' subliminally. By drawing lessons from experience, it is possible to apply one's earlier knowledge in a new format to new problems. This is what creativity means.

To get his business running, Hans drew on previous experience. He had been mesmerised by how his former employer, a pearl merchant, made profits yet *creating nothing*. From this employer, Hans learned an invaluable lesson on how one can *draw strength from competent sources* (outsourcing). He outsourced most of his production. Thus, having little or creating nothing in material terms can still be turned into something of value when one has a definite and worthy cause. Outsourcing, as a competitive strategy or model, is not in itself the key, but one's ability to harness the capacity of outsourcing by creative or imaginative means in a right manner can help one to avoid exploitation.

In the early 1980s, Nike, the world-renowned sport-kit firm, was already known for outsourcing to the Far East but, in the Nineties, rather than continuing to gain market share, sales began to plummet and profits were on a downward trend, until the Air-Jordan factor came to the rescue. Michael Jordan, a basketball mega-star, was contracted for endorsement as the face of Nike.

The company had employed this technique before with other stars, but now it became very relevant because this was during a critical moment of societal anger against Nike for outsourcing. After the Michael Jordan contract, the company (founded by Phil Knight and Bill Bowerman while full-time employees with other entities), regained strength and became unstoppable.

In a similar fashion to the introduction of Michael Jordan and other stars to Nike, the Rolex Oyster, the single most important brand of Hans's business, became popular due to the Mercedes Gleitze's factor. Mercedes, a very competent swimmer, wore the watch around her neck while attempting to swim the English Channel in 1927. She was repeating her attempt because an earlier, successful attempt had not been well received or gained much publicity among the general public. Her story, on this second attempt, was one of triumph in defeat, but it still helped break Hans Wilsdorf's business frontier because Mercedes won the adulation of a wider community. A month after her swim, Hans rigorously promoted and advertised the Oyster with her heroic story.

Unsurprisingly, it seems that most businesses now follow this path. They outsource but also allow for creativity in the form of creative celebrities added to their teams (stars or other promotional title bearers such as musical talents – Will.i.am for Intel, and Alicia Keys for Black Berry).

However, those who seek to benefit from this trend must be sure to add a new perspective as did Hans. Hans took charge of what matters most – the quality-assurance of his watches. Quality has been described as 'continuous improvement in inputs, processes and outputs'. By adhering to continuous improvement as a personal ritual, Hans developed competitive muscles and obtained a pioneering reputation for quality for his company. Those individuals who maintain continuous improvement in thoughts and actions can build their confidence and their unique individual identity or authority can be improved or upgraded. Tom Peters, a renowned management consultant, once concluded, in relation to work and business, that: '*excellent firms don't believe in excellence* – only in constant improvement and constant change'.

The road to personal discovery is thus embedded in cleaving to your personal guides and rituals. Personal guides – or a personal philosophy – were described in Chapter 8. Every successful individual or innovative organization (those that make available their creative streams to the market) has always abided and held to definite rituals. For example, to perfect their skills, Ben Feldman and Ericson (*see* Chapter 8) always stayed two hours longer at work beyond the usual office time.

Wole Soyinka, the first Nobel Laureate from Africa, is credited with writing at any time and everywhere. It still seems like mystery that a man who was refused books, papers and pens could yet publish some of his work while incarcerated.

But commitment to rituals can and should be combined with other factors. For instance, while on mission for his employer (ritual), Tom Peters sought for what drives excellence in businesses (passion), and to describe one of the things he observed he coined the expression, 'Management by Wandering Around' (MBWA) (exploit), which, to a lay person, means nothing but to entrepreneurs and business leaders means substance.

Tom Peters learned this idea from a company that was quite small by the standards of that period, *but he did not despise it for its smallness.* From smallness and what others might call almost nothing, he made his contribution to organization management. In a manner similar to that of Napoleon Hill, who also contributed while on a mission for his employer (ritual), new light shone on Tom (exploit) and gave birth to a new mission for him (passion). He dreamed again and, in pursuit of his dreams, set up his own firm.

All this group of individuals found a passion and committed

themselves by rituals and exploited their passion by continuing to dream creatively and innovatively.

Dreams develop in this fashion: passion – ritual – exploit.

Dangers lurk if ritual does not follow passion. Huntingdon Life Science, an animal testing service, almost capsized recently because some employees were cruel to the dogs in their care and refused to adhere to what the organization had garnered its strength from: the ritual of listening and responding sensitively to peoples' views, feedback and then review, had been the hallmark of the company's success and had helped it to grow to become one of the leading non-clinical contract research organizations in the world.

People must be appreciated because, ultimately, they are the stuff that dreams are made of. It is important to remember that in fulfilling one's dreams, and regardless of how colourful and glamorous a vision one has, it is necessary to seek the cooperation of one or two trusted hands be they consultants, delegates, associates, mentors or a quality-circle of team mates as is Japanese practice.

If you consider great organizations and innovations that withstood the test of time, the founding founders did not act all alone. An obvious example would be the working relationship that existed between Bill Gates and Paul Allen when Microsoft started. Again, Warren Buffett achieved economic recovery for one of his businesses owing to his exceptional reliance on a turnaround Manager, 'Harry the Bottle' after previous managers did not live up to his expectations. Again, Goldman Sachs survived the depression era of the Twentieth Century, dreamed again and rose to become a premier Investment bank on a global scale courtesy of the ingenuity of Sidney Weinberg, one of the company directors. The list of working partnerships could be continued almost *ad infinitum*.

If you can't teach an old dog a new trick, at least, they should be listened to. Many individuals or businesses concentrate on meeting new friends, prospects and customers but, often, success or failure is dependent on feedback (usually complaints) from known customers or other 'partners', be they internal (workplace colleagues) or external. In like manner, whether a dreamer is good or less than good, most extraordinary dreamers really take flight for the top only after bearing the brunt of others' anger, mockery or complaints. Face can be lost temporarily in the presence of accusers but, to ensure that this has little or no effect, one needs to dream again.

Having overcome several hurdles in their careers and having

fostered their employers' interests in terms of growth and profit, both Joe Girard (a salesman of extraordinary ability) and Charles M. Schwab (the first President of United States Steel Corporation) were technically laid off at the peak of their careers so far, owing to company politics. Both dreamed again. Joe attained the topmost height of his career with a new company selling a higher number of automobiles than any other known individual or dealer in the world. Charles's recovery was even more impressive.

After being forced to resign, he developed a number of small businesses with his managerial insights to the extent that the competence of these businesses as a group (Bethlehem Steel Corporation), rivalled those of his former employer.

It is important that, no matter how daring a dreamer may be, he/she should not delight in high-risk activities for the sake of it, nor tangle with excessive and uncontrollable debts, a problem that has characterised the latter days of a number of dreamers with numerous achievements, including notable musicians, doctors, inventors, and even, Charles M. Schwab.

To make big dreams become real and to dream again when all one has seems to be nothing, is to stand tall against competition *by aiming beyond it*. If one stands tall with good thoughts, great actions can spring from small means. In order to stand tall, smallness in thought must give way to greatness of vision.

This is the essence of little lights: to dream again, one must take charge – because dreams *do* come true.

Chapter 10

Footprints

Love fulfils.

Terry Fox raised $24.17 million for the cause of Cancer Research in 1981. In 2014, Stephen Sutton raised more than £4 million for the same cause. The legacy left by these two men is of more consequence than simply the very obvious support that they garnered while fundraising. In their last moments on earth, these men showed that love strengthens and supersedes all things, they fell in love with their lives and cherished their last days with friends and loved ones. Every second was treasured more than gold, the tiniest electromagnetic device could not detect any trace of depression in them and both of them got engaged in recreational activities that many would consider strenuous. Because of this, their strength amazed the world. Even after death, the cause they stood for outlived them and their memory serves as a source of inspiration to all of us to value life while it lasts.

Life is full of numerous challenges and, as individuals, we, at one time or another, will also have been dealt with blows from life – but identifying a worthy cause to stick with through thick and thin can help drain from us a lot of the mental stress that life inevitably creates. A testament to this must be Oprah Winfrey's success, well-known across the world.

On this earth, the only planet we have, after health, peace and wealth, the other things that bring comfort are: finding a purpose, being a success and being happy. But all of these come in many forms. To many, for instance, the process of finding a purpose means asking themselves what career path they can derive satisfaction from, or asking which field best aligns with their talents, dreams and ambitions, or which job can better help pay the bills. In these instances, life revolves around an unending stream of targets and achievements and a worthy cause that centres on others is not found and followed and thus the problems remain at some level.

No longer should the centrepiece of our lives be, 'when will the next big story happen?' Rather, we should remember and consider the words of Thich Nhat Hanh, a well-revered

Vietnamese Buddhist monk: 'The miracle is not to walk on water. The miracle is to walk on the green earth, dwelling deeply in the present moment and feeling truly alive'.

Aristotle is said to have claimed that to attain the ultimate good, which is happiness, one must live a life of virtue. Interestingly, while virtue may involve numerous different philosophies and the actions that arise from them, Cicero asserts that, 'gratitude is not only the greatest of virtues, but the parent of all others' which is perhaps a rather odd idea to modern ears but worth considering.

One of the lessons that most successful high schools teach their students is that they should not forget their *alma mater* if they become successful. This is no bad idea. Also, do not forget to appreciate what matters most. Generally, people say thanks to their friends, family and even government by giving gifts or service and paying tax. If we do all these, which at times are not convenient, but are mandatory as tuition fees are to the paying students, what then can we willingly do as a form of gratitude to life itself, bearing in mind that a person's lifetime is a sort of school as described in Chapter 1? What can we willingly bring to our world in terms of meeting others' needs, following a worthy cause or strengthening other valuable systems with our talents, passions and dreams?

Jim Loehr, the founder of the Human Performance Institute, has assisted notable and distinguished individuals such as Andre Agassi, former world-no-1 tennis player, and Gene O' Kelly, former KPMG pacesetter. In several encounters with clients, Jim has coped with challenging times. He has been a strong advocate of aligning one's goals and personal achievement to a worthy cause. He, like other great minds, has also noticed that this approach can bring joy to numerous individuals. Money, jobs or achievements thus change from being 'an end in themselves' to being 'a means to an end' when a worthy cause is followed.

Across the nooks and crannies of the world, the footprints of many of the virtuous are felt even before they leave this planet. For instance, we can't talk of the Internet today without being aware of the scientists, engineers and entrepreneurs who have been involved in its evolution. Fred Terman of Stanford University was one of them. He worked hard on transistors or semi- conductors. Silicon Valley can't be much talked about without mentioning the semi-conductor business that grew with it from a small start-up city.

And we can't talk about the silicon valley and all that invention and entrepreneurial ingenuity (at the start, the little township lacked capital and was despised by its wealthy eastern counterparts) without mentioning Arthur Rock, a man whose life revolves around helping others find meaning, be it in technology, education, medicine or business. It has been said of him, 'he invests in people and not ideas". Widely acclaimed as a man who shuns popularity contests but has genuine interest in people, he is known to have helped many with the little things of life, and from this a large number of people around the world enjoy the benefits. This is a virtue worth mentioning.

A virtue is such as an attitude of appreciation towards life, and it takes the form of selflessly finding and following a cause, for example, by helping an orphanage, by volunteering for green issues, and other such altruistic endeavours. It thus can be an everlasting source of joy and satisfaction to the individual. Andrew Carnegie, one of the richest men that ever passed through this world, found his cause in helping the self-development of others and contributed huge sums of money to the funding of libraries across several continents.

Business establishments have also embraced this noble

concept. Chris Bartlett of Harvard Business School and Sumantra Ghoshal of the London Business School have both observed that firms that defy threat from imitation are those that strengthen their core business proposition through a mission that surpasses the rather obvious fundamentals of profit-making. These firms give back to others through the development of valuable personal relationships with their clients and by a social policy that sees to the comprehensive well-being of their employees and the environment.

After writing this chapter, I learned of Tony Lobes, a South African Engineer whose story also exemplifies the essence of it. Using bottles and tins, Tony employed his engineering talent to create plastic-bottle skylights and other similar inventions that offer solutions for the less privileged in South Africa. These highly valuable (in the real sense of the word) goods are being produced at a LOw-cost, and the idea emerged, according to him, from a quote he learned from Albert Einstein: 'put back into the Earth at least what you took out of it'. His story can be found on TEDx's platform (Technology, Entertainment and Design).

This Earth, the only planet we call our own, cannot erase the footprints of those who gave of their substance to it while they passed through her.

Thank you for devoting your time to studying
this little book of lights.

Bibliography
and further reading

Chapter 1

Dejoria, J.P. (2011). "Success Unshared is Failure" *The CEO Forum*. Issue 3

Jones, F. A. (1908) *Thomas Alva Edison: Sixty Years of an Inventor's Life*. New York: Cromwell and Co. Publishers. Pg 9.

Low, K. C (2013) "Are you MAD enough? If not, how would you have grown your career?" *Educational Research* Vol. 4 (6) Pg. 499.

Putnam, M. (1974). "Three Philosophical Poets by George Santayana". *Daedalus* 103 (1). Pg. 131.

Tracy, B (2002) *The 100 Absolutely Unbreakable Laws of Business Success*. California: Berrett-Koehler Publisher. Pg 14.

http://archive.org/stream/thomasalvaedison00jonerich/thomasalvaedison00jonerich_djvu.txt

http://www.techfaster.com/homeless-hacker-leo-grand/

Chapter 2.

Neal, J. (2013) *Alcoholics Alive!* Indiana: iUniverse Books. Pg 505.

Kaswell, E., (1999). "The Transition from Silk to Nylon for Parachutes During World War II". *Textile Chemist and Colorist and American Dyestuff Reporter.* 1 (2).Pg 36

Turngate, M., (2008) *Fashion Brands: Branding Style from Armani to Zara.* London: Kogan Page Publishers Pp 197-200

http://www.itv.com/news/2013-11-19/philippines-village-celebrates-miracle-storm-shelter/

Chapter 3.

Khan, S. (2012) *The One World School House: Education Reimagined.* London, Hodder and Stoughton Limited. Pp. 1-20

Montgomery, B., (1958). "The Montgomery Memoirs: Part 3. Bulge, Bitterness, but Final Victory" *Life. 45 (17).* Pg 82.

The Eisenhower Foundation (1999*). Dwight D. Eisenhower-Dreams of a Barefoot Boy:1890-1911.* Kansas: The Eisenhower Foundation Pg 28.

Thierer, D. (1994) "Unnatural Monopoly: Critical Moments in the Development of the Bell System Monopoly". Cato Journal 14 (2), pp. 267-285.

Yunus, M. and Jolis, A. (2003) Banker to the Poor: The Story of the Grameen Bank London: Aurum Press Limited. Pg 5-6

Chapter 4

Pelta, K. (1991) *Discovering Christopher Columbus: How History is Invented*. USA: Lerner Publications Company.

http://www.bloomberg.com/video/90012489-bloomberg-game-changers-magic-johnson.html

http://www.ok.co.uk/celebrity-news/the-x-factor-2013-sam-bailey-told-shell-sell-records-on-great-british-songbook-week

http://www.shakespeare-online.com/plays/julius_2_2.html

Chapter 5

Anionwu, E. (2012) "Mary Seacole: Nursing Care in Many Lands." *British Journal of Healthcare Assistants*. 06 (05). Pp 244-248.

Drucker, p. (1985). *The Effective Executive*. New York: Harper Collins Publishers

Ghandhi, M. (1922) *Ethical Religion*, Madras: S. Ganesan Publishers. Chapter 6, pg. 61

Leahy,T. (2012) *Management in Ten Words. London: Random House Business Books.*

Miller, D. (2008) *No More Mondays: Fire Yourself – and Other Revolutionary Ways to Discover Your True Calling at Work.* The Doubleday Broadway Publishing Group. Pg 52.

Winkelstein, W. Jr. (2009) "Florence Nightingale: Founder of Modern Nursing and Hospital" *Epidemiology*. 20 (2): 311.

Whitman, M., Hamilton, J. (2010). The Power of Many: Values for Success in Business and in Life. New York: Crown Publishers.

http://www.achievement.org/autodoc/page/bez0bio-1

http://web.archive.org/web/20071031084056/www. historycooperative.org/btw/Vol.7/html/235.html.

http://www.success.com/article/morris-goodman-miracle-man

http://www.theguardian.com/lifeandstyle/2009/feb/01/mo-ibrahim

http://www.ziglar.com/quotes/zig-ziglar/your-ability

Chapter 6

Kleege, G. (2000) Helen Keller and "The Empire of the Normal" *American Quarterly* 52 (2): 322-325.

Kelsey, F. (1988). "Thalidomide update: Regulatory aspects". *Teratology* 38 (3): 221–226.

Lund-Wilde, J (2011). "The Story behind Harry Potters Magic" *ejournals.bc.edu > Home > Vol 13, No 3 (2011).Access:* http://www.bbc.co.uk/news/magazine-16907648

Mason, J. (1990) *An Enemy Called Average.* USA: Insight Publishing Group.

Neimark, A. E. (1970). *Touch of Light: The Story of Louis Braille.* Harcourt, Brace & World.

Weis, D. (2010) *Everlasting Wisdom- Your Ultimate Quoter with The Wittiest Ever Said About Almost Everything.* UK: Paragon Publishing, Rothersthorpe.

http://www.forbes.com/sites/stevedenning/2014/08/02/a-tribute-to-warren-bennis-a-leader-of-leaders/

http://www.huffingtonpost.com/2011/05/07/chinese-artist-huang-guof_n_858833.html

http://www.independent.co.uk/news/obituaries/rosala-mera-seamstress-who-accrued-a-fortune-as-cofounder-of-zara-8773289.html

http://www.telegraph.co.uk/culture/books/authorinterviews/9968921/Love-in-the-time-of-cornrows-Chimamanda-Ngozi-Adichie-on-her-new-novel.html.

http://www.thisdaylive.com/articles/yinka-ayefele-what-the-president-s-handshake-did-to-me/138188/

http://www.tomyendell.co.uk/

http://www.victorianweb.org/authors/dickens/diniejko.html

http://www.warrenbennis.com/images-home/Ch_1.pdf

Chapter 7

Carnegie, D. (2004). *How to Stop Worrying and Start Living.* USA: Simon and Schuster Inc.

Dessauce, M. (1999). *The Inflatable Moment: Pneumatics and Protest in '68.* New York: Princeton Architectural Press. Pp 17.

Edison, T. (1908). *Sixty Years of an Inventor's Life* by Francis Arthur Jones, p. 14. *Accessed*: ttp://archive.org/stream/thomasalvaedison00jonerich/thomasalvaedison00jonerich_djvu.txt

Ezekiel, G. (2012). *Sachin: The Story* of *the* World's Greatest Batsman. UK Penguin Books.

John11: 50-54

Marden, O. (2007). The Wisdom of Orison Swett Marden: How to Succeed, an Iron Will, and Cheerfulness as a Life Power, Volume 1. USA: Wilder Publications. Pg 180.

Matthew 10: 16.

Matthew 4:12-13

Rose, M. (2003). *The Staff of Oedipus: Transforming Disability in Ancient Greece*. Michigan: University of Michigan Press. Pp. 50-52

Senge, P. M. (1990). *The Fifth Discipline: The Art and Practice of the Learning Organization*. New York: Doubleday/Currency.

Skolnik, F., Berenbaum, M. (2007). "Eilshemius Louis". *In Encyclopaedia Judaica, Volume 6* Granite Hill Publishers Pg 255.

Worthington, I. (2012). *Demosthenes of Athens and the Fall of Classical Greece. New York:* Oxford University Press

http://news.investors.com/management-leaders-in-success/103000-349621-ges-jack-welch-can-do-attitude-helped-him-climb-to-the-top.htm

http://planetearth.nerc.ac.uk/news/story.aspx?id=637

http://thoughtokrats.com/pdffiles/Leadershipdevelopment/Jackwelch%27sLeadershipStyle.pdf

http://www.arctictern.info/carsten/results.html

http://www.bbc.co.uk/history/historic_figures/van_gogh_vincent.shtml

http://www.iupac.org/publications/ci/2011/3301/jan11.pdf

http://www.lairweb.org.nz/leonardo/mona.html

http://www.michelin.co.uk/about/history

http://www.theguardian.com/lifeandstyle/2009/feb/01/mo-ibrahim

http://www.visionrescue.org.in/viewNavMenu.do?menuID=7

Chapter 8

Bleier, T., and Steinert, E. (2000). *Net.people: The Personalities and Passions behind the Web Sites*. New Jersey: Cyber Age Books.

Hampson, R. (1993). The Extra ordinary Life of a Salesman. *The Victoria Advocate Saturday, Nov 27, 1993*. Pg19.

Parton, D. (1994). *Dolly: My Life and Other Unfinished Business*. 1st Edition. UK: HarperCollins Publishers.

Rotary International (1969). *1969 Proceedings: Sixtieth Annual Convention of Rotary International*. Rotary International. Pg. 185

Smiles, S. (1859). *Self-Help with Illustrations of Conduct and Perseverance*. London: John Murray.

Weismann, A. (1889). *Essay upon Heredity*. Oxford: Clarendon Press Pp. 421-448

http://www.ericssonhistory.com/company/a-different-company/Ericsson-and-911/

http://www.nps.gov/history/logcabin/html/al1.html

http://www.scientificamerican.com/article/day-the-web-was-born/

http://www.statista.com/statistics/241828/number-of-visits-to-ikea-stores-worldwide/

http://www.well.com/conf/inkwell.vue/topics/132/Derek-Powazek-Design-for-Communi-page01.html

http://www.yueno.jp/bits/index.html

Chapter 9

Burton, M. (2013). *The 3-Ships of Success: The Powerful Connectivity of Three Tenants of Business.* USA: iUniverse.

Buffett, M. and Clark, D. (2010). *Warren Buffett's Management Secrets: Proven Tools for Personal and Business Success.* London: Simon-Schuster-Ltd.

Geoffrey, J and Atzberger, A. (2013). "Hans Wilsdorf and Rolex." *Harvard Business School Case 805-138, May 2005. (Revised).*

Hessen, R., (1990). *Steel Titan: The Life of Charles M. Schwab.* USA: University of Pittsburgh Press.

Hill, N. (2009). *The Master Key to Riches.* USA: Dover Publications.

Kauffmann C. (2010). *Kauffmann Index of Entrepreneurial Activity.* Kauffmann Foundation.

Orwell, G. (2004). Penguin Great Ideas: Why I Write. London: Penguin Books. Pp 4-5.

Peters, T. (1987). *Thriving on Chaos: Handbook for a Management Revolution.*

New York: Harper Business.

http://nikeinc.com/pages/history-heritage

http://online.wsj.com/news/articles/SB100014240527023
04441404579119742104942198

http://thenextweb.com/entrepreneur/2014/04/24/kevin-rose-says-wishes-stayed-ceo-digg/

http://www.economist.com/node/13216025

http://www.forbes.com/sites/clareoconnor/2014/01/31/10-things-you-didnt-know-about-microsoft-billionaire-paul-allen-seattle-seahawks-owner/

http://www.inc.com/magazine/20081101/keeevviin.html

http://www.joegirard.com/

http://www.newyorker.com/magazine/2008/11/10/the-uses-of-adversity

http://www.thecqi.org/The-CQI/What-is-quality/

http://www.theguardian.com/environment/2006/nov/22/
freedomofinformation.animalrights

Chapter 10

Bartlett, C., and Ghoshal, S. (2002). "Building Competitive
Advantage through People." *MIT Sloan Management
Review* 43 (2): 34–41.

Gupta, U. (2000) *Done Deals: Venture Capitalists Tell Their
Stories*.USA: Harvard Business School Press.

Loehr, J. (2012). *The Only Way to Win: How Building Character
Drives Higher Achievement and Greater Fulfilment in Business
and Life Hardcover*. New York: Hyperion.

Nhat Hanh, T. (1996). *Be Still and Know: Reflections from
Living Buddha, Living Christ*. New York: The Berkley
Publishing Group.

http://www.thepsychologist.org.uk/archive/archive_home.
cfm?volumeID=20&editionID=143&ArticleID=1129

समाप्त

Made in the USA
Monee, IL
17 March 2026

46281836R00090